ITALIAN PLEASURES

Italian Pleasures

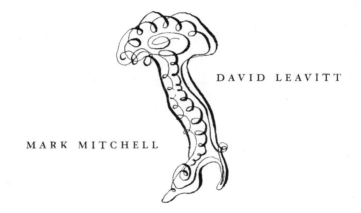

DAVID LEAVITT

MARK MITCHELL

FOURTH ESTATE • *London*

First published in Great Britain in 1996 by
Fourth Estate Limited
6 Salem Road
London W2 4BU

To maintain the authentic style of each writer included
herein, quirks of spelling and grammar remain unchanged
from their original state.

A catalogue record for this book is available from the British
Library.

ISBN 1-85702-589-X

Text design by Pamela Geismar
Text illustrations by Elvis Swift
Printed and bound in Great Britain by
Biddles Limited, Guildford and King's Lynn

To Alessandro Bartolomeo Marazzi Sassoon

"… it is a strange sensation for me to keep company with people who live only for pleasure."

—Goethe, *Letter from Naples (March 16, 1787)*

ACKNOWLEDGMENTS

Andrea Bacchi (Florence), Alberto Battisti (Florence), Berta and Andrea Bucciarelli (San Gimignano), Manuela and Rand Burkert (Spello), Fausto Calderai (Florence), Paolo Fiume (Florence), the late Sir John Pope Hennessy (Florence), Louis Inturrisi (Rome), Michael Mallon (Florence), Cosimo Manicone (Florence), Giovanna Marazzi and David Sassoon (New York), Mina and Goffredo Marazzi (Milan), Gabriele Pieraccini (Cesena), Pina, Giampaolo and Martino Pingi (San Martino sul Fiora), Marco Pupo (Florence), Mark Roberts (Florence), Michael Rocke (Florence), Emily Rosner and Maurizio Panichi (Florence), Antonio Tanca (Brussels), and Cira and Luisa Volpe (Florence).

Contents

E. M. Forster, among the most discerning of travel writers, came to Italy for the first time in 1901, with his mother, and his experiences in and of the "exquisite peninsula" found their way into two of his novels, *Where Angels Fear to Tread* and *A Room with a View*. For him, Italy was more than the triptych Rome, Florence, and Venice—he knew (and wrote about) the small towns as well. Still, even the generous and perceptive Forster perpetuated some Anglo-Saxon myths of the place. In *Where Angels Fear to Tread*, for example, Philip Herriton tells his sister-in-law, Lilia, "Love and understand the Italians, for the people are more marvellous than the land." And in *A Room with a View*, the lady novelist Eleanor Lavish exclaims to Lucy Honeychurch, when they come upon a picturesque wine cart, "How the driver stares at us, dear, simple soul!"

Well, Italians are a marvelous people, as Forster and we and many others have experienced, but they also can be as rude and insular and self-interested and hypocritical and xenophobic as anyone else. Sometimes, then, with apologies to Forster, the land *is* more wonderful than the people. And whatever the Italians are, they are not "simple."

The first enduring novel about Americans in Italy was Nathaniel Hawthorne's *The Marble Faun*. The Yankee sculptor Kenyon has gone to see his friend Donatello in Tuscany, and when he discovers that his friend's life is not an idyll, he confesses,

> I have fancied you in a sort of Arcadian life, tasting rich figs, and squeezing the juice out of the sunniest grapes, and sleeping soundly, all night, after a day of simple pleasures.

The Anglo-Saxon "fancy" that all Italians do is eat spaghetti, and drink red wine, and sing opera, and make love, and dance the *tarantella* under perpetually blue skies, is understandable: there must be a place in the world where life is happy. And yet, how much more complex and rich is Italian reality.

In our reading, most books written about Italy have not managed to be just: the tendency is either to praise overmuch everything under the Italian sky (which the sky over no other country in the world can match), or to be sour and condescending about the same everything. *Italian Pleasures*, then, is not a book about charming undiscovered hotels, which, rather than for the hardness of their mattresses, guides recommend for their adorableness; not a book about how wonderful or how awful Italy is. Italy is both, because it is a real country, and not

fairyland (even though, now and again, it is just possible to believe that it might be fairyland). So, for the
pleasure of Italian light, there is the displeasure of
Italian pollution; for the pleasure of Italian coffee,
the displeasure of having to buy bottled water
because Italian tap water is frequently undrinkable;
for the pleasure of living among magnificent buildings and ruins, the displeasure of negotiating the
masses of tourists who come to photograph them;
for the pleasure of ordered Italian gardens, the displeasure of chaotic Italian politics; for the pleasure
of two- or three-hour Italian lunches, the displeasure of late Italian trains. The nineteen excerpts
we have chosen to include from the works of other
writers on Italy articulate pleasures as sometimes
heterodox as our own.

When this book was in the planning stages, we
managed a list of fifty or sixty Italian pleasures that
we could, or might, write about. Since then, quo-
tidian life has demolished some of the pleasures on
that first list, and probably this is all to the good; we
would have been "taken in" by the superficial—
which true pleasure can never be. "There is no short
cut," as Edith Wharton once wrote, "to an intimacy
with Italy." These are the pleasures, then, of a lived,
not a visited, Italian life, and if, in spring, we

remember the first time we came here, full of innocent ardor for the place, and feel sad for that state,
we will also understand what an Italian poet once
told us about innocence: it is a good thing to have,
and a better thing to lose.   — M.M.

*T*he traveler arrives late at the station. Train strikes, delays: no one ever gets to Italy on time.

"I'm here."

"Great. Where is here?"

"At the station, actually. In ———. Or rather, below ———, since at the moment the town is hovering over me like a vision of heaven in a painting of purgatory—"

"Spare me the description, I'll be there in ten minutes."

His friend, the resident, hangs up, the traveler thinks, with surprising ferocity, no doubt fatigued by such tourist poetry. He takes off his raincoat. He's standing on an empty platform in a tiny station in the middle of a plain. Above him, on its hill, ——— looms and shimmers. Pale green meadows leap to greet it. The air has a yellowish cast, as if the sun has melted and been absorbed into the fabric of the sky.

In the bar, an indolent red-haired girl arranges coconut slices on a three-tiered revolving tray: listlessly, listlessly trickles of water pour from a spout at its tip, then spill over the staggered tiers. In every bar in every station in Italy there is such a tray, and in every one of them coconut slices are what it displays, though the traveler, in all his journeys to that country, has never seen a single person actually buy one.

Italy, he thinks. Somewhere else. And waits, in jet-lagged somnolence, to be fetched.   — D.L.

A friend of ours grew up in the Isle of Capri trailer park in South Carolina, and though the name had nothing to do with the magnificent island in the Bay of Naples it had everything to do with the desire almost all people have to live in a place that acknowledges the existence of the beautiful. And what a beautiful place is Capri. To read in a guidebook that eight hundred kinds of flowers grow here is no substitute, no preparation, for seeing eight hundred kinds of flowers: gardens composed only of rose and cactus, and fumaroles of bougainvillea. A restaurant near the *Arco Naturale* serves grilled buffalo-milk mozzarella on a white plate covered with leaves from a lemon tree, the way to the Villa Fersen is lined with poppies and nasturtium, and in the heat of summer days lavender and rosemary perfume the steep walk down to the sea near the three *Faraglioni*. Finally, there is the Mediterranean; cold and profound and glittering— one shade of which colors the acute eyes of the Capriotes.

Capri seems like many other places—its narrow walks remind me of Venice, the style of architecture of Palm Beach, the sheer cliffs of the *Monte Solaro* of

Yosemite, the older men and their kept boys of Fire Island, the winding Via Krupp of Lombard Street in San Francisco, the small bakeries of Salzburg—but what makes it unique and whole is color. Most things in human life are notable for their physical colors (holidays, uniforms, ceremonies) and for each of these I can think of—the red and green of Christmas and the orange of Halloween, the blue and yellow of Cub Scout uniforms, the white of weddings—Capri has its equivalent: red and green are the colors of hibiscus blossoms and foliage and orange that of Lantana; blue and yellow those of the *Grotta Azzurra* and clematis; white that of honeysuckle flowers.

All this is to say that Capri reminds the visitor, through color, of all he has ever known and all he will ever know. After coming here, can fuschia ever be anything other than those petals that seem made of brittle Japanese paper and that hang like days on the wall of the little square in the center of the island?　　　　　　　　　　　　　　　— M.M.

Each June the village of Spello, just around the hill from Assisi, celebrates its annual *infiorate*, or dried flower festival. Here is what happens: the night before the *infiorate* the men and women of the town, having divided into groups, begin tracing chalk outlines (planned months in advance) on the pavement of the piazza and surrounding streets. Meanwhile children and old widows in black sit on the sidelines in wooden chairs, separating by color dried and fresh petals: *fiori del melograno* (pomegranate flowers), *garofolini* (sweet william), *ginestrella* (greenweed), *tagete* (marigold), cedar of Lebanon, rose, *fiordaliso* (cornflower). Boxes and boxes of color, deep golds like curry powder, royal blues, hot pepper reds, that as dusk approaches the *Spellini* begin, very carefully, to scatter inside the traced outlines. (The color scheme, like everything else, has been long foretold.) Until dawn Spello is an enormous coloring book, in which nature provides the crayons. (Strict rules prohibit dyeing or in any other way artificially enhancing the petals.) Then, around seven in the morning, the *infiorate* are finished.

The most elaborate *infiorata* features actual newspaper headlines about the war in Bosnia, a slaughtered lamb, and, in white and blue, some bars from Beethoven's *Ode to Joy*. Every detail is flawlessly executed, so much so that from a distance you'd swear the picture was drawn with chalk. Another *infiorata* recounts the plight of the American Indians. A third brings together the emblems of the principle world religions: Buddha, the Koran, a Torah, and a Bible. None of the petals are glued down; instead, to keep them from blowing away, the tired-looking *Spellini* must pace all day alongside their *infiorate*, dampening them with water.

In the afternoon prizes are awarded; the *infiorate* are faithfully photographed. Finally at dusk everyone goes home, relinquishing their labors of a year, accepting the inevitable demolition that the wind, the streetcleaners, the tromping feet of tourists will insure.

Sometimes the *Spellini*, in their zeal to achieve, each year, new levels of technical excellence, forget that artistry is needed to bring craftsmanship alive. It is a little bit sad (especially this close to Assisi, where Giotto painted) to see such immense mastery as they have achieved resulting only in sermonizing and sentimentality. Then in a corner I encounter three little girls who have made of their petals the simplest image of all: flowers (why not?) accompa-

nied by a white cross. These little girls in red, yellow, and green jumpsuits kneel next to their work,
faces full of—no, not pride; instead a kind of odd
embarrassment, stubbornly proprietary without
being in the least gloating; what I can only call the
true artist's nervous devotion, wincingly conscious
of flaw, yet nonetheless unwilling to abandon a work
that, for all its inadequacy, is still a child, illuminates
the faces of these little girls.   — D.L.

D.L. — It is the overabundance, the excess, of Italy that amazes the foreign visitor. D. H. Lawrence recorded the amazement of his wife Frieda, the "queen bee" (or q-b) of *Sea and Sardinia*, upon visiting a Cagliari vegetable market.

We went down to the little street—but saw more baskets emerging from a broad flight of stone stairs, enclosed. So up we went—and found ourselves in the vegetable market. Here the q-b was happier still. Peasant women, sometimes barefoot, sat in their tight little bodices and voluminous, coloured skirts behind the piles of vegetables, and never have I seen a lovelier show. The intense deep green of spinach seemed to predominate, and out of that came the monuments of curd-white and black-purple cauliflowers: but marvellous cauliflowers, like a flower show, the purple ones intense as great bunches of violets. From this green, white, and purple massing struck out the vivid rose-scarlet and blue crimson of radishes, large radishes like little turnips in piles. Then the long, slim, grey-purple buds of artichokes, and dangling clusters of dates, and piles of sugar-dusty white figs and sombre-looking black figs, and bright burnt figs: basketfuls and basketfuls of figs. A few baskets of almonds, and many huge walnuts. Basket-pans of native raisins. Scarlet peppers like trumpets: magnificent fennels, so white and

big and succulent: baskets of new potatoes: scaly
kohlrabi: wild asparagus in bunches, yellow-budding
sparacelli: big, clean-fleshed carrots: feathery salads
with white hearts: long, brown-purple onions and
then, of course pyramids of big oranges, pyramids
of pale apples, and baskets of brilliant shiny man-
darini, the little tangerine oranges with their green-
black leaves. The green and vivid-coloured world of
fruit-gleams I have never seen in such splendour as
under the market roof at Cagliari: so raw and gor-
geous. And all quite cheap, the one remaining
cheapness, except potatoes. Potatoes of any sort are
1.40 or 1.50 the kilo.

"Oh!" cried the q-b, "if I don't live at Cagliari
and come and do my shopping here, I shall die with
one of my wishes unfulfilled."

———————

D. H. Lawrence, *Sea and Sardinia* (1921)

The first time I came to Italy alone, I lacked the knack for meeting strangers. Once in Bologna, out of desperation, I tried to have a chat with the stout *padrona* of my pension, who happened to own a little Pekingese dog. Although I could speak only two sentences in Italian—"*per favore, parla inglese?*" and "*per favore, parla francese?*"—I thought to myself, the word for dog in French is *chien;* and since Italian words are basically French words with an "a" on the end, I pointed to the animal and said, "*cena?*" at which point the woman's eyes bulged in horror as she grabbed the beast protectively to her breast.

As I learned later, *cena* means dinner.

This was by no means the last of the mistakes I made in Italian; in fact, ten years later, when I'd actually studied and begun to learn the language, I started making even more. Once in Sestri Levante, for instance, my friend Giovanna and her very correct Milanese parents and I were talking about the various resort towns near Genova, one of which is called Chiavari. "*Ti piace Chiavari?*" I asked Giovanna's mother, who went white. Later, Giovanna explained to me that by mispronouncing "*Chiavari*" as *"chiavare,"* I had asked her mother if she liked to fuck.

Mistakes go in the other direction, too. A charming example of awkward translation is the English menu we were handed at one of those places one goes to once. In this case the imaginative author, knowing that *primi piatti* means "first courses" and *secondi piatti* "second courses," sensibly rendered *antipasti* as *"course d'oeuvres."*

Finally this: Italians (like Spaniards) have great difficulty hearing the difference between certain English words: "chip" and "cheap" sound almost identical to their ears; so, too, "pip" and "peep," or "dip" and "deep." Thus you can imagine the surprise of an Italian friend when he went to an American supermarket and found a toilet paper roll that proclaimed "1000 SHEETS."

"America is a wonderful country," he said.

— D.L.

*A*ll paper money is a pleasure, of course, but Italian paper money has the right spirit: the people on it are not dreary politicians. These days, Maria Montessori (founder of the schools) is on the 1,000 lire note (Galileo is on the older ones); Marconi (inventor of the wireless) on the 2,000; Bellini (the Sicilian composer of bel canto operas) on the 5,000; Volta (the physicist in whose honor the volt is named) on the 10,000; Bernini (the sculptor) on the 50,000; and Caravaggio (the painter) on the 100,000.

In sum, the currency of Italian culture is Italian culture.   — M.M.

Q had to go to the post office to pay the water bill—never much fun in Italy, since Italians have not yet caught on to the idea of waiting for the next available teller. Because there are as many lines as there are tellers, all you can do is hope—pray—that you don't get stuck behind someone intent on making trouble. As it happened, I chose the wrong line. The man in front of me got into a heated argument with the teller because she wouldn't accept his torn fifty thousand lire note. Italian notes have a metallic strip sewn into them to distinguish the real from the forged; in this man's case, the strip was not intact.

Discussion quickly escalated to the level of fight. Not that it needed to—the man brandished a billfold stuffed with fifty thousand lire notes; the problem was that he was determined to pay his bill with this *particular* fifty thousand lire note.

Oh great, I thought, and eyed the other lines, running smoothly. Customers who'd arrived just when I had were already leaving. I started to fume. And then a strange thing happened. As the voices of the man and woman rose to a pitch just below shouting, I found myself becoming increasingly hypnotized by their elaborate—almost arcane—rhetoric. Something primal, historical, was being fought out here. Perhaps he was Guelf, she Ghibelline; he black, she white. It occurred to me that argument could be a form of intimacy, a ritual as elaborate as the mating dances performed by exotic birds. Vendetta—the settling of a score—was not its purpose; its purpose was the brandishment of rhetorical *epées;* the venting of spleen.

As is inevitable in such situations, a supervisor was soon demanded, produced. While he listened to the man's plaint a finger of ash formed on the end of his cigarette. A lady near the back of the line interjected that just yesterday the post office had accepted a bill of hers that was in worse condition. (The teller's eyes narrowed: traitor.) The man started shouting at the supervisor. The supervisor shouted back. Then, just when blows seemed certain to ensue, the tension, as it were, deflated; the protagonists, descending from icy heights, reached sudden and complete accord. A new note was produced (the old one to be turned in at the bank). Good wishes were offered round like after-dinner mints. The customer was *molto gentile* ("very nice"), the teller *troppo gentile* ("too nice"). The supervisor prayed that should the gentleman have any further problems he would come directly to him, and the gentleman, promising to do so, wished him a *buona giornata*, as if to say, rest assured: this argument was just a game; all the days and evenings will puddle into a happy and profitable life. — D.L.

FIREWORKS

*T*he Italians are a noise-loving people, particularly fond of the noise of bad television. "Voices hoarse and shrill" that raise "tumult and pandaemonium"—such as Dante heard in the *Inferno*—make a karaoke show broadcast from a different Italian town each night one of the most popular programs in the country. When we first began watching *Karaoke*, it was hosted by Fiorello, but the mantle has now passed to Fiorellino (or "Little Fiorello"), his younger brother. (Fiorello, incidentally, is so famous that when his penis was injured as a result of someone pushing him into a wall while he was peeing against it, a Livorno newspaper put it on the front page. It is possible, of course, ethics being no barrier to entertainment in Italy, that the story was just that.)

Fireworks are also popular; they—the fireworks—belong to the secular and to the ecclesiastical equally. We have watched the *fochi* in Florence on the feast day of San Giovanni, the city's patron saint, and were in St. Mark's Square, in Venice, for the fireworks one New Year's Eve: jubilant explosions lifted into splendor the shawl-like fog that clung to the brittle shoulders of that superannuated queen of Italian cities. — M.M.

M.M. — Michelangelo's *David* is, one supposes, the most famous sculpture in the world. Among the chief impediments to his appreciation, however, is his omnipresence as both tourist attraction and tourist artifact. Walter Pater writes of the marble from which Michelangelo made *David*.

[Michelangelo] loved the very quarries of Carrara, those strange grey peaks which even at midday convey into any scene from which they are visible something of the solemnity and stillness of evening, sometimes wandering among them month after month, till at last their pale ashen colours seem to have passed into his painting; and on the crown of the head of the *David* there still remains a morsel of uncut stone, as if by one touch to maintain its connexion with the place from which it was hewn.

Walter Pater, *The Renaissance* (1873)

Pigeons have caused some lovely moments in the Italian world: it was not blossoming pear trees or Giotto's frescoes that touched me the most in Assisi, but rather a forlorn pigeon, its left wing mangled; it was the torrential orbit of a thousand pigeons that (except for this sound) made the Piazza della Signoria in Florence the quietest place on earth one day; not David, not Judith, not Perseus had ever done so much to astonish the place into silence.   — M.M.

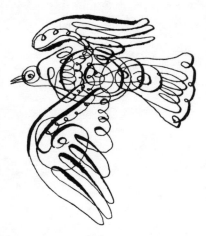

NOCTURNE

Late at night, in the Piazzale degli Uffizi, in Florence, one sometimes hears the blues played on a saxophone. The echo of that music, in that place, is otherworldly. The sooty graces in the Loggia dei Lanzi and the herms beside the doors of the Palazzo Vecchio, as much as the very real lovers kissing by the river, seem to listen; suspended in the amber of serenity and patience and happiness.

— M.M.

M.M. — I am told that Nellie Melba (*née* Helen Porter Mitchell) is, very distantly, among my ancestors. In her memoirs, the famed soprano tells the story of a woman whose love for Venice was so great that she moved an actual Venetian *palazzo* to Boston. (Today that *palazzo* is the Isabella Stewart Gardner Museum.)

Mrs. Jack Gardner was, in many ways, my *beau ideal* of what a rich woman should be. I don't know how many millions Mrs. Gardner had—probably she did not know herself—but whatever their fortune, it was spent in the service of beauty. To some extent Mrs. Gardner occupied the position in the United States which Lady de Grey held in London, and certainly no other woman in America could possibly have conceived the stupendous plan of bringing over from Europe an entire Venetian Palace and setting it up, stone by stone, in Boston, Mass.

She was in the middle of this vast enterprise when I met her, and she was naturally full of excitement. Every stone of the palace had to be numbered and checked. Every precious piece of carving had to be packed in shavings and preserved from careless hands. Even the Italian plants in their original pots, filled with Italian earth, made that perilous journey across the Atlantic and arrived, by some miracle, to flower under a foreign sun.

Of course I was longing to see "It" as she always described her palace, but "It" was sternly guarded from all prying eyes until it was finished. Nobody, not even the President of the United States, would have been allowed to enter. Everything, inside and out, had to be perfect before Mrs. Gardner would share her treasure with the world. Meanwhile we had to be content with rumours of what was going on inside, of which one of the most prevalent was that a certain Italian prince was lingering in prison for allowing one of his pictures to be smuggled out of Italy on consideration of £40,000.

Then one day, the summons came. Mrs. Gardner rang me up on the telephone. "It's finished," she said, a note of triumph in her voice, "and you're going to be one of the first people to see it. May I call for you in my brougham this afternoon at three o'clock?" Needless to say, I accepted.

It was a bitterly cold afternoon when we set out for the palace, with a blizzard blowing at sixty miles an hour. Imagine therefore my delight when we arrived, and two tall Italian servants opened the door, to admit us to an exquisite garden full of spring flowers. For the courtyard of the Palazzo had all been roofed in with glass so that, even in winter, one could have Italian flowers and a very fair counterfeit of Southern warmth.

A room which she called the "Van Dyck" room was one which immediately captured my attention. It was of immense size, with a tall roof which even in the day-time was shrouded in shadow. At night it was lit with hundreds of candles, and the first effect one had on entering it was that of darkness so thick that none of the pictures could be seen. However, one had not been in that room five minutes before every picture became clearly visible in its smallest detail.

People talked about Mrs. Gardner, of course, as they talk about anybody who takes the trouble to undertake a really big job. They said for example that it was affectation for her to carry her passion for detail so far as to insist on the letters being handed up in a basket each morning, as is done in Venice. Finding that she did not in the least mind this criticism they went farther, and when they heard of her marvellous painted ceilings, said that the pictures on them were so improper that she had been forced to hide them in the roof.

But she took no notice—this great little woman—but went on her way with the true fervour of the aesthete (that much abused word). One picture of her will always linger in my memory—that of the little ceremony with which she always preluded her dinner parties. Imagine a long Italian gallery, dimly lighted, with white statues, glimmering on either side, and a hint of marvellous pictures in the dusk. We all gather at one end of the gallery and then Mrs. Gardner—a tiny figure in white draperies—lights a taper. Very slowly she walks down the gallery in silence, while we wait, past the statues into the distance, and then we see her gravely light two little candles in front of an altar at the far end.

Nellie Melba, *Melodies and Memories* (1925)

In old photographs of Naples laundry crosses the narrow streets almost festively. Clothes naturally look better hanging outside a seventeenth-century palazzo than a twentieth-century high-rise, yet Italian clothes hang with a certain timelessness, almost even with a consciousness that clothes are for the most part a custom rather than a utility. (This is why Italian fashion is so marvelous: it has nothing to do with necessity.) And so the underwear of old women and the socks of adolescent boys dry, ebulliently, in that precarious world of shutters and geraniums and ocher walls and cats and terra-cotta and Madonnas that breathes above the old streets.

— M.M.

I remember also the dialect of the city of
Naples, which is Italian chewed to shreds in the
mouth of a hungry man. It varies even within the
city. The fishermen in the bay talk differently from
the rich in the Vomero. Every six blocks in the
squashed-together city there's a new dialect. But the
dialect is Naples and Naples is the dialect. It's as raw
as tenement living, as mercurial as a thief to your
face, as tender as the flesh on the breast. Sometimes
in one sentence it's all three. The stateliness of
Tuscan Italian is missing in Neapolitan. But there's
no false stateliness in Naples either, except in some
alien fountain presented by a Duchess of Lombardy.
Neapolitan dialect isn't ornamental. Its endings have
been amputated just as Neapolitan living pares to
the heart and hardness of life. Wild sandwiches
occur in the middle of words, doublings of *z*'s, cram-
ming of *m*'s and *n*'s. When they say something, the
Neapolitans scream and moan and stab and hug and
vituperate. All at once. And O God, their gestures!
The hand before the groin, the finger under the
chin, the cluckings, the head-shakings. In each sentence they seem to recapitulate all the emotions that
human beings know. They die and live and faint and
desire and despair. I remember the dialect of Naples.

It was the most moving language I ever listened to. It came out of the fierce sun over the bleached and smelly roofs, the heavy night, childbirth, starvation, and death. I remember too the tongues that spoke Neapolitan to me: the humorous, the sly, the gentle, the anguished, the merciful, and the murderous. Those tongues that spoke it were like lizards warm in the sun, jiggling their tails because they were alive.

John Horne Burns, *The Gallery* (1947)

ats abound in Roman archaeology. You don't notice them at first; indeed, only after you've focused your vision for awhile do you start to pick them out: a gray one is licking its paw among the ruins in Largo Argentina; a calico missing an eye is crouched on a pediment in the gladiators' quarters near the Colosseum. Three, four. You keep counting. Nine, ten, twenty. Dozens of cats, more cats than people: yet hushed, woven into the landscape.

One wet May afternoon I took a walk over the Campidoglio and down through the park of Monte Caprino. A carpet of plum blossoms, soaked to a pulp, gave off a nauseating perfume. A cat with a beauty mark perched under a pine, its expression livid as it waited out the storm. Altogether the hill pulsed with a feline silence usually unknown to the

urban landscape. In the absence of human noises—
the squeak of tennis shoes, the crack of cigarette
lighters, the staticky swish of coats being slung over
shoulders—other sounds became audible: you could
actually hear the scratchings of a small cat, all white,
as it buried its feces in a flowerbed; you could actually hear pinecones falling, or grass bending under
the weight of rain.

That afternoon I learned silence. Habitually a
noisy person—loud voice, stomping feet, thrashing
gestures—I sat still as a cat on a bench and gazed
at a ledge where some good soul had put out a green
plastic dish of the sort usually used to catch the run-
off under a planter, filled with broth and pasta. As
the afternoon straggled on rain diluted the broth
until it spilled over the edges. Now and then cats
came and licked at it. Even the dipping of their pink
tongues I could hear. Even the brush of their soft,
wet tails against the mossy stone I could hear in that
rare, even sacred silence.   — D.L.

There is as much (and sometimes more) to learn in the Catholic church by keeping one's eyes on the terrestrial as by keeping one's eyes on the celestial. For example, into the floor of St. Peter's Basilica in Rome are set the names and measures of Christendom's great churches; from St. Peter's itself—the largest—down to St. Patrick's in New York.

Templum Vaticanum
Londinense.S.Pauli.Fanum
Florentina.Metropolitana
Ecclesia SS.Cordis Jesu Bruxellis
Sanctuarium Immaculatae Concept.Washington
Ecclesia Cathedralis Rhemensis
Templum.Cathedrale.Coloniense
Primarium.Templum.Mediolanense
Ecclesia Cathedralis Spirensis
Basilica.S.Petronii.Bononiae
Templum.Metrop.Hispalen.Sevilla
Basilica Metrop.B.M.V.Parisien
Basilica.S.Pauli.Via.Ostiensi
Ecclesia.Cathedralis S.Viti Pragae
Primatialis Ecclesia Toletana
S.S.Ecclesia.Lateranensis

Ecclesia Cathedralis Metropolitana Mexicana
Eccles.Cathed.B.M.V.Antverpiensis
Eccl.S.Iustinae.V.M.Patavin
Basilica Cathedralis Esztergom
Ecclesia Cathedralis Ferrariens
Basilica Assisien.S.Mariae Ang.
Cath.Metrop.Sancti Pauli Brasilia
Ecclesia Cathedralis Westmonasteriensis
Constantinopolitana Divae.Sophiae.Ecclesia
Basilica Gedanensis Beatissimae Virginis Mariae
Ecclesia Metropol.S.Patritii Neo Eboracen

Each church seems to have been fitted into the one before it; so many Chinese boxes.　　— M.M.

      arly in the Tuscan summer, bright yellow posters start appearing all over the city advertising a *sagra* of tortelli and wild boar to be celebrated in the town of Ronta.* Usually sponsored by local branches of the Communist party, the *sagra* is a venerable institution in which the eating of some delicacy—truffles, porcini mushrooms, cherries, tripe—is combined with dancing, games, the sale of remaindered books as well as lectures on such appetizing subjects as financial law, "satire and art," and the relationship between tumors and the environment. (In Italy, communism is pink, not red.)

The sight of this poster stirs my memory, because the first *sagra* we ever went to was also in Ronta, a small town near Borgo San Lorenzo, in the Mugello hills. On a public playing field endless picnic tables had been set up under tents. The atmosphere was one of jocular festivity verging into violence: colorfully decked-out women ran back and forth, bearing wild boar meat on plastic plates; their husbands filled old water bottles with acrid-tasting wine; in the

---

* *Tortelli* is the name for the kind of ravioli, filled in the Mugello hills with mashed potato, of which *tortellini* are the smaller and *tortelloni* the bigger versions.

enormous tented kitchen grandmothers boiled up *tortello* after *tortello*, stirred immense kettles of *ragù*; the young people screamed and sang and ate.

Of the Italians, Edith Templeton remarked to a friend: "I cannot make them out; they seem to be so much happier than the other nations I know." This was in the years just after the Second World War, when the country was paying for its allegiance to Mussolini. "We are happy for no reason at all," Mrs. Templeton's friend told her, "and it is a very pleasant state to be in. Now, what is it you want to know?"

I cannot help but think about this bit of dialogue when the *sagra* posters, faithful as the first figs, start to appear. If the word *sagra* derives from the same root as our word "sacred," there is a lesson to be learned from the etymology. In Italy, the *rite*, in its most pagan form, is sacred. And when, at any *sagra*, a boy of alarming beauty alights from a table populated exclusively by boys of alarming beauty, and his friends shout "Where are you going?" it is no surprise to hear him answer, "To vomit!" as he disappears cheerfully into the night. The Roman orgy is not far from us here.   — D.L.

*O*ne rainy Sunday, with my brother, we drove south from Florence to Monteriggioni, where it began to clear, then on to Pienza. There we came upon a *Festa di Primavera* and in the shade of a tent, we ate lunch: the best *ribollita* (a Tuscan bread and vegetable soup) any of us had ever tasted, fresh local pecorino and fresh *baccelli* (fava beans), *porchetta*, delicate raw artichokes dipped in hazy olive oil. For dessert, we each chose an ice cream at a café with a ceiling of shivering wisteria.

All of this happened by default. Pienza's principal restaurant, recently written up in *La Cucina Italiana*, was completely full that day. Had it not been, we would never have gone to the spring festival.

Later, as we were walking back to our car, we saw the young man from the restaurant whose duty it had been to send away all those who had not made reservations buying a ticket for his own lunch under the billowing shadows of the festival tent.   — M.M.

*O*ur Garzanti Italian-English dictionary defines *checca* as "gay, fairy, pansy, queen." None of these translations is quite accurate, however. Yes, a *checca* is by definition a flaming, theatrical homosexual, but the word lacks the nasty bite of its English equivalents: more often than not, it is used simply as a nominative, a way of identifying someone without judgment.

A friend who has lived thirteen years in Rome tells the following story: one morning he went to see the owner of his local *vivaio*, or nursery, about a sprinkler system. The owner, as it happened, had a pet crow that flew around the shop shrieking irately. "*Smettila, Checca!*" he shouted in irritation: "put a lid on it, you pansy!" "I wasn't sure if he was talking to the bird or to me," our friend said.

Afterwards, he asked the owner of the *vivaio* why he called the bird *checca*. "*Ma guarda,*" the owner said, gesturing. Our friend looked at the crow as instructed and had to agree. "It had all these *feathers* ..."

In Rome, *la checca* is also a pasta dish very popular in the summer months: penne or rigatoni served with raw tomato, garlic, mozzarella, *peperoncini*, and fennel seeds. (*Finocchio*—fennel—means the same thing as *checca*.) According to our friend, at Roman markets one often sees next to bins of San Marzano tomatoes a sign identifying them as being *per la checca*. Since our local market stall lacked such a sign, Mark shyly asked which tomatoes to use for this dish. (Also, we wanted to find out if our friend was making it up.) "*Questi*," the *fruttivendolo* answered, and pointed casually to some ripe red *pomodorini* from Calabria.

"La Checca"

To make *la checca* you need a pound of Italian short pasta (rigatoni is best), a couple of pounds of ripe red tomatoes, a head of garlic, two dried hot peppers, good olive oil, salt, fennel seeds, fresh basil, and mozzarella. Only make this dish in summer, when tomatoes are in season, and only use tomatoes that are red and juicy.

Peel the cloves of garlic, score them with a knife, put them in a big bowl, and add the olive oil, the chopped tomatoes (skinned and seeded if you're feeling ambitious), the fennel seeds, the *peperoncini*, and some salt. Let the whole marinate for three or four hours; over the course of this time the salt will draw the juice from the tomatoes as well as the flavor from the garlic, creating a heady *sugo*. While cooking the pasta remove the *peperoncini*. Cook the pasta and toss it with the tomato mixture, adding at the last minute some fresh basil leaves and the mozzarella cut into cubes.   — D.L.

D.L. — Joseph Forsyth's description of the water gardens at Frascati dates from his visit to Italy in 1802 and 1803. Today the garden still can be toured, as can others like it, in Bagnaia (Villa Lante), Caprarola (Villa Farnese), and, most famously, Tivoli (Villa d'Este).

———

From Tivoli I made an excursion to Frascati, to view the Tusculan villas, which are still as conspicuous and as white as of old. At present Prince Borghese is the Lucullus of the hill; for the three largest of its palaces, Mondragone, Taverna and Belvedere, belong to that family.

Belvedere commands most glorious prospects, and is itself a fine object, from the scenic effect of its front and approaches. Behind the palace is an aquatic theatre formed by a stream which flows from Mount Algidus, dashes precipitately down a succession of terraces, and is tormented below into a variety of tricks. The whole court seems alive at the turning of a cock. Water attacks you on every side; it is squirted on your face from invisible holes, it darts up in a constellation of *jets d'eau*, it returns in misty showers, which present against the sun a beautiful Iris. Water is made to blow the trumpet of a centaur, and the pipe of a Cyclops; water plays two organs; makes the birds warble, and the Muses tune their reeds; sets Pegasus neighing, and all Parnassus on music. I remark this magnificent toy as a specimen of Italian hydraulics. Its sole object is to surprize strangers, for all the pleasure that its repetitions can impart to the owners is but a faint reflection from the pleasure of others. The Borghesi, I understand, seldom visit the place.

———————

Joseph Forsyth, *Remarks on Antiquities, Arts and Letters During an Excursion in Italy in the Years 1802 and 1803* (1813)

*I*f there had not been a New Testament, there would not be so many pictures in the Uffizi Gallery. Yet for the seriousness of the ever-ramifying themes, there is great and surprising life as well. The right panel of a Mantegna triptych depicts the circumcision of Christ: Joseph is present, and Mantegna has shown him holding his robes where his genitals are—a gesture any man watching a circumcision would be likely to make. And in a painting by Veronese of the Holy Family with Saint Catherine and Saint John, the sleeping baby Christ holds his penis—an act of comfort and pleasure. The human ordinariness of such reactions and such actions is not profane; indeed, the works are more sacred for them.

Life always, whether the picture be religious or secular: the Christ in a Botticelli Madonna holds a pomegranate; in a Bronzino portrait, a grinning boy (destined to die of malaria) holds a bird; the Virgin marks her place in a book to attend the archangel who has interrupted her reading in a da Vinci; a Bacchus stays from his grapes to leer in a Caravaggio; the Madonna is painted with a fancifully long neck by Parmigianino (so that the picture

is called *The Madonna of the Long Neck*); and
Federigo di Montefeltro, Duke of Urbino—in Piero
della Francesca's splendid portrait—is painted moles
and all.   — M.M.

*O*ne of my favorite places in Florence is the tiny chapel in the Palazzo Medici-Riccardi, where Benozzo Gozzoli painted his frescoes of the procession of the Magi. In this narrow, odd-shaped chamber every inch of every wall is rife with life. As much is going on in the frescoes as in the hidden picture drawings I used to pore over as a child, and indeed, much of the pleasure of standing there is childish: the delight of noticing startling little details for the first time (a greyhound playing with some ducks); the sense of immersion in an alternate world that, covering every wall, literally envelopes. And Gozzoli has left nothing out. In addition to the many men and women and children who make up the procession—several modeled on prominent Florentine citizens—there are the animals: dogs, deer, birds, pheasant, monkeys; and there are the precise, enigmatic trees—umbrella pines, cypresses (also like umbrellas, but closed ones), and that tree peculiar to Renaissance painting the foliage of which rises up in staggered even tiers, like the metal platters that display coconut slices at station bars.

Of all the animals, my favorites are the two leopards that gambol amid the gentry. Exceptionally beautiful, they are the size of large housecats, with the mouths and whiskers of gryphons. Their expressions suggest both sweetness and wisdom. Most curiously, the spots that cover their gray coats appear to form tiny *fleurs de lis*. It's as if they've been upholstered in Pineider paper.

A very elegant woman I used to know had two identical black cats that slept symmetrically atop the symmetrical stacked pillows on her bed—almost as if they were pillows themselves. I could imagine Gozzoli's leopards doing something like that. (Oscar Wilde, in his "art for art's sake" period, would have approved of such animals.) It's as if even nature has recognized the supremacy of Florence (the symbol of which is, of course, the *fleur de lis*). Indeed, I suspect Gozzoli never saw an actual leopard, but based his specimens on written descriptions, or a bestiary: a drawing of a drawing of a drawing.

The dogs attract me as well, but for the opposite reason: because they resemble so closely the real dogs I encounter when I take walks through the Piazza della Signoria: little tenacious mongrels, some with underbites, beige with beige noses, or liver-colored, or the color of dirty sheets. Their tails beat like hummingbirds as they frolic amid the tunicked legs of knights (one purple, one white), or chase birds, or tangle the horses. They are beautiful because they embody the essence of canine being: familiarity, the intimate knowledge of the house-holder, brings them alive. — D.L.

*O*f the Protestant cemetery in Rome, where are interred the ashes of Shelley and

all that was mortal,

of a

YOUNG ENGLISH POET

—Keats ("Here lies One Whose Name was writ in Water")—Axel Munthe wrote in *Memories and Vagaries*, "The grave is not the dark abode of corruption, polluted by the decay of the body. The grave is the urn wherein the memory of a human soul is laid."

I went there on a bright warm morning. One does not usually think of cemeteries as consoling places, but this one is. Some of the resident cats were lapping milk that had been left for them in the opening of the wall along the Via Caio Cestius. A pair of kittens accompanied me on my walk, now running ahead, now pausing to mew, now doubling back to rub themselves against my ankles. Two middle-aged women sat on a bench in the *parte antica* and chatted, while in the small kitchen of the cemetery offices, the custodian made a salad of tomatoes and mozzarella—a pleasure I interrupted when I bought

a guide from him. The Cestius Pyramid (first century B.C.) shone platinum among ilex and myrtle, rose, narcissus, hydrangea, ivy and violet, and sweet summer grass. Beyond the walls, the sounds of the eternal city.   — M.M.

———

One begins to realise how old the real Italy is, how man-gripped and how withered. England is far more wild and savage and lonely, in her country parts. Here since endless centuries man has tamed the impossible mountain side into terraces, he has quarried the rock, he has fed his sheep among the thin woods, he has cut his boughs and burnt his charcoal, he has been half domesticated even among the wildest fastnesses. This is what is so attractive about the remote places, the Abruzzi, for example. Life is so primitive, so pagan, so strangely heathen and half-savage. And yet it is human life. And the wildest country is half humanised, half brought under. It is all conscious. Wherever one is in Italy, either one is conscious of the present, or of the mediaeval influences, or of the far, mysterious gods of the early Mediterranean. Wherever one is, the place has its conscious genus. Man has lived there and brought forth his consciousness there and in some way brought that place to consciousness, given it its expression, and, really, finished it. The expression may be Proserpine, or Pan, or even the strange "shrouded gods" of the Etruscans or the Sikels, none the less it is an expression. The land has been humanised, through and through: and we in our own tissued consciousness bear the results of this humanisation. So that for us to go to Italy and to *penetrate* into Italy is like a most fascinating act of self-discovery—back, back down the old ways of time. Strange and wonderful chords awake in us, and vibrate again after many hundreds of years of complete forgetfulness.

D. H. Lawrence, *Sea and Sardinia* (1921)

One August night I walked up to the Forte di Belvedere to see an exhibit called *Firenze e le sue immagine*: "Florence and its Images." The Belvedere is on a hill behind the Pitti Palace, and that evening the view from it was more exquisite than any view in it. I caught light and color at their most intense: navy and lavender earth, black cypresses, rose and flame and della Robbia blue sky, oxblood imbricated roofs, parmesan-colored lights wobbling, in bewildering heat, across the valley towards Pisa.

And my mother, when she came here the October before, observed that even on the rainiest and grayest of days the warm colors many of the buildings are painted—cream, mustard, saffron, butterscotch, egg yolk, zabaglione—give the impression of sun upon them. — M.M.

I have a memory of Mantua in the fog: driving through the plains of Emilia, the fog rising from ordered fields wet as rice paddies; then the city with its eel-filled lake, its narrow streets that the fog itself seems to navigate, vaporous and heady as the steam rising from a pasta pot. The people of Emilia call London *"la città nebbiosa"*—the city of fog—and yet I've never seen any place so foggy as Emilia in early winter. We eat ravioli filled with pumpkin in a restaurant where the light is as white and brittle as a Ginori plate, then tour the immense Gonzaga Palace with its apartment for the court dwarves, its *Camera degli Sposi* from the ceiling of which Mantegna's *trompe l'oeil* angels peer down with ageless curiosity. Even here the fog can be felt as a dim, moist, grayish light: a wetness to the walls, outside of which run moss-choked canals, breeding ground to carp a hundred years old.

Yes, I remember Mantua in the fog. And yet isn't memory itself a fog, shrouding, obscuring, distorting, softening, so that I will never be sure how much of the fog I remember is real, how much composed from memory itself?   — D.L.

D.L. — You can no longer climb to the top of the Leaning Tower of Pisa. This is because over the last century the tower has become more eccentric each year, making entry dangerous. In this passage, Mark Twain offers a vivid account of what it was like to see the world's most famous monument from the inside.

———————

At Pisa we climbed up to the top of the strangest structure the world has any knowledge of—the Leaning Tower. As everyone knows, it is in the neighborhood of one hundred and eighty feet high—and I beg to observe that one hundred and eighty feet reach to about the height of four ordinary three-story buildings piled one on top of the other and is a very considerable altitude for a tower of uniform thickness to aspire to, even when it stands upright, yet this one leans more than thirteen feet out of the perpendicular. It is seven hundred years old, but neither history or tradition says whether it was built as it is purposely or whether one of its sides has settled. There is no record that it ever stood straight up. It is built of marble. It is an airy and a beautiful structure, and each of its eight stories is encircled by fluted columns, some of marble and some of granite, with Corinthian capitals that were handsome when they were new. It is a bell tower, and in its top hangs a chime of ancient bells. The winding staircase within is dark, but one always knows which side of the tower he is on because of his naturally gravitating from one side to the other of the staircase with the rise or dip of the tower. Some of the stone steps are footworn only on the one end; others only on the other end; others only in the middle. To look down into the tower from the top is like looking down into a tilted well. A rope that hangs from the center of the top touches the wall before it reaches the bottom. Standing on the summit, one does not feel altogether comfortable when he looks down from the high side; but to crawl on your breast to the verge on the lower side and try to stretch your neck out far enough to see the base of the tower makes your flesh creep and convinces you for a single moment, in spite of all your philosophy, that the building is falling. You handle yourself very carefully all the time, under the silly impression that if it is *not* falling, your trifling weight will start it unless you are particular not to "bear down" on it.

Mark Twain, *The Innocents Abroad* (1869)

*T*hese are not the best days for Italian fashion, the critics say; still, the windows of the
big designer shops are always something to see. In
Florence, the one I like best is Luisa Via Roma.

It has become something of a local tradition to
insure that one's evening walk (or Sunday afternoon
passeggiata) takes one past Luisa Via Roma, which is
found between the Piazza della Repubblica—the
ugliest in town (without a fountain, without a statue,
without a tree)—and the octagonal Baptistry. There
are two windows, and each of the principal sexes gets
its own: boys the left, girls the right (the larger of
the two).

It is a pity the boy mannequins are so shopworn—not to mention so unmasculine—because
they do detract from the clothes in which they are
clad. One's lips are quite chipped, in fact, and his
chain mail vest and white patent leather shoes exalt
him to a state of intense pathos. The men's department is up a spiral staircase at Luisa Via Roma, and
though there are some beautiful designs by Donna
Karan (among others), the windows always go for an
effect and tacitly criticize any man that does not have
an Italian build and a preference for castrating

underwear: the pants are always long and tight and high-waisted, and would under no circumstances permit boxer shorts to be worn beneath them. Once, the mannequin wore—with an effort towards rakishness—a top hat made from steel mesh: the only thing on the boy side that has ever tempted me. There is no such thing as a window screen in Italy, and the idea occurred to me that I might deconstruct the hat and make of it a screen for our bedroom since in summer the choice is either to keep the windows closed and suffocate (yet be free of mosquitoes) or to open them and be bitten (and good).

The girl window has six or seven mannequins, and they enjoy the tremendous benefit of being arranged—unlike the boys, who, being boys, just stand around ill at ease—in *tableaux*: caught in the rain, with glass droplets falling from the ceiling; chatting, as if at a cocktail party; or in attitudes suggesting the Muses, or the Graces. The clothes they are put in look better than those given to the boys, too: in fact, it is a rare window in which I do not see an outfit or two that I would like to have.   — M.M.

*I*talian boys do something better than any other boys in the world: they lean, and they do it against walls, against Vespas, against each other. Italian bodies seem to fall naturally and spontaneously into beautiful *contrapposto:* the S curve of sculpture. It is beautiful because it is physical, if not active: it is an event in its own right.

Hawthorne made much of the faun of Praxiteles (in Rome), and most people have made much of the Michelangelo and Donatello Davids. (Theophile Gautier was an admirable holdout, describing Michelangelo's as looking like "a market-porter.") But no sculpture of an Italian boy is so wonderful as a living, leaning Italian boy: how difficult it is not to be like the driver of the "adorable wine-cart" in *A Room with a View*, and stare.

Even the famous bell tower in Pisa does not lean so well.   — M.M.

I get out at Parma. My idea of Parma is Edwardian, derived from tales of my mother's youth.

Parma means Parma violets, a large bunch of them pinned to a lady's fur. The garment is a stole or a cape. And the fur from which it is made is, of course, chinchilla. Already in my childhood it was a legendary fur, almost extinct. I saw it on only two occasions, when it had the shabby nobility of an old Rolls-Royce. But its name had a whispering, sibilant enchantment recalling the rustle of taffeta petticoats, the crunching of sugared almonds.

Those were the days of *demi-mondaines*, and I imagine that those ladies used to wear huge compositions of Parma violets, fastened with a long slim brooch set with a single black pearl, arranged on an ivy leaf and with the stems wrapped in silver paper. The decent women wore bunches of a modest size.

Parma violets could be worn one day only, because they lost their fragrance when put into water. They were the true flowers of lavishness.

Edith Templeton, *The Surprise of Cremona* (1954)

*I*n a cave at Cumae, near Naples, a woman lies in a cage hung from a hook. She is incredibly old; barely sentient; an atom of life that if you rock the cage shivers a little; otherwise you would never recognize it as life; you would think it was just a speck of dust.

Ovid tells the story this way: in her girlhood the woman—her name was Sibyl—was courted by Phoebus, who for love offered her anything she might desire. Pointing to a heap of dust some unknowing domestic had swept together in the corner, Sibyl asked if she might have "as many birthdays as there were grains of dust"; but she forgot to ask for eternal youth as well. Of course Phoebus recognized her rash mistake, and offered her eternal youth too—if she would sleep with him. She refused, and presumably as punishment, Phoebus not only failed to make the necessary amendment, he also failed to withdraw the tainted gift.

Sibyl got older and older, and became a prophetess, gaining fame when she guided Aeneas on his journey through the Underworld. Then she started to get too old. According to Petronius drunken revelers and children would stumble into her cave to look at her, now reduced to the size of a cicada. "Sibyl, what do you want?" they would ask her, and she would answer, "I want to die." But she didn't die. She outlived Phoebus himself. Even now she endures, as tiny as one of the grains of dust that started the trouble in the first place.

I sometimes think I ought to tell this story to Professor R. except that I doubt he would understand its relevance.

A portly American in his sixties, Professor R. has eked out a living teaching English in Italy for thirty years now. I cannot imagine what he looked like in his youth. Perhaps he was beautiful. (Phoebus also sometimes fell in love with beautiful boys.) But now his cheeks bear that perpetual flush that is the legacy of too much drinking. His teeth are bad. He wears bifocals that slide slowly down his red nose as he talks.

I go to dinner with him one night. Also at the table are another professor of English and an eminent translator. There is wine. They start talking about Italian girls, which provokes Professor R. to start talking about Italian boys. "In Lecce, you find the most beautiful boys on the peninsula," he tells us. "And all of them quite amenable to whatever you propose."

"Really," says his colleague, evincing that anthropological interest the heterosexual libertine often takes in the doings of his homosexual counterpart.

"Yes. You don't even have to pay. Quite marvelous. I can't tell you anything about the girls. In Sicily they're lovely, I'm told. I wouldn't know. I've never had the slightest interest in girls. I do adore Sicilian boys. My companion is Sicilian. Giuseppe. An orphan. He came to live with me when he was seventeen. He's quite exquisite. Would you like to see?" A snapshot is passed around. "Such muscles! Giuseppe goes every day to the gym. But we don't make love anymore. That aspect of our relationship has faded with time. We are friends now. Not that it matters, because I've found a lovely Romanian boy. He comes over every Saturday night, I cook him a good dinner, we make love, I give him some money. It's an ideal arrangement. I'm very happy. And in the summers, I travel: to Puglia, to Calabria. I spend all my time with the boys. Imagine, a sixty-three-year-old man like me, and always with boys! That's the wonderful thing about our kind. We never grow up."

Our dinner companions, having listened to this monologue in silence, announce they must be going: wives are waiting, children are waiting. Never have the comforts of home beckoned more urgently! And really, they will tell their wives when they get home, it is a tragic thing to be an old pouf.

As for me, I recognize myth when I see it.

Professor R.'s fate is the opposite of the virginal Sibyl's: he has been granted eternal youth without eternal life. — D.L.

M.M. — Hawthorne had this to say about Italy:

> religion jostles along side by side with business and
> sport, after a fashion of its own; and people are accus-
> tomed to kneel down and pray, or see others praying,
> between two fits of merriment, or between two sins.

The Pantheon is the very symbol of a people divided
between the pagan and the Christian: built to honor all
the gods—and this meaning is given in its name—it was
converted into a Christian church in the seventh century.
All the same, it is a pagan building, no matter the addition
of an altar, or even the tomb of Raphael. Above the bronze
doors of the Pantheon, mounted on their sill of green
African marble, is this inscription:

> *INDULGENTIA.PLENARIA*
> *QUOTIDIANA.PERPETUA*
> *PRO.VIVIS.ET.DEFUNCTIS*

Words, except Marguerite Yourcenar's in *Memoirs of
Hadrian*, do not do it justice.

On the same day, with graver solemnity, as if
muted, a dedicatory ceremony took place inside the
Pantheon. I myself had revised the architectural
plans, drawn with too little daring by Apollodorus:
utilizing the arts of Greece only as ornamentation,
like an added luxury, I had gone back for the basic
form of the structure to primitive, fabled times of
Rome, to the round temples of ancient Etruria. My
intention had been that this sanctuary of All Gods

[64]

should reproduce the likeness of the terrestrial globe and of the stellar sphere, that globe wherein are enclosed the seeds of eternal fire, and that hollow sphere containing all. Such was also the form of our ancestors' huts where the smoke of man's earliest hearths escaped through an orifice at the top. The cupola, constructed of a hard but light-weight volcanic stone which seemed still to share in the upward movement of flames, revealed the sky through a great hole at the center, showing alternately dark and blue. This temple, both open and mysteriously enclosed, was conceived as a solar quadrant. The hours would make their rounds on that caissoned ceiling, so carefully polished by Greek artisans; the disk of daylight would rest suspended there like a shield of gold; rain would form its clear pool on the pavement below; prayers would rise like smoke toward that void where we place the gods.

Marguerite Yourcenar, *Memoirs of Hadrian* (1951)

*T*he most beautiful pictures of umbrella pines are Neapolitan gouaches: in the foreground, the pine itself; in the midde distance, costumed Southerners dancing the *tarantella;* in the far distance, the Bay of Naples. These are the pictures that answer the idea of perfect place, which in art really does exist; and perhaps—-in the past—existed in life.

Unfortunately such pictures, when they can be found, are very dear: I came upon one in a shop on Via dei Condotti, the street that sweeps with such superb aplomb up to the Spanish Steps in Rome, that cost three million lire. Too much, because these gouaches, most of the them painted in the nineteenth century, have the most fragile of surfaces. With the passage of time, gouache begins to powder, and so in a miniature way the fragility of a city that has been, and might one day be again, destroyed by Vesuvius, is echoed in these paintings of it. (George Gissing, who traveled to Southern Italy in 1897, wrote, "Vesuvius to-day sent forth vapours of a delicate rose-tint.... The cone, covered with sulphur, gleamed bright yellow against cloudless blue.")

There is a secret untruth in these Neapolitan pictures: beneath the gouache is blue board, for this intensifies the color of sky and sea. But untruth is essential for getting at the truth—the true blue—of sea and sky.

Most Neapolitan gouaches are unsigned (the *firma* of the artist raises the price into the stratosphere), which makes their anonymous inventiveness all the more eloquent: I have seen a gouache painted on the blue cover of an Italian school notebook from the Fascist period; a view of Vesuvius, sailboats lolling in the bay, painted on an ivory piano key; Posillipo, by night, painted on the surface of a mirror.

One day, perhaps, I shall find an affordable version of the painting with, in the foreground, the pine itself; in the middle distance, costumed Southerners dancing the *tarantella*; in the far distance, the Bay of Naples. If I do, I will spirit myself into it, lean my back against the pine, and look across into blue.

— M.M.

*S*ince settling in Italy, we've made it our habit to spend Christmas at the thermal spa in Saturnia, soaking in the mineral waters with their delicious stink of sulfur. We also play the *tombola*, an Italian version of Bingo that, because it is Italian, you can win in many more ways than you can win at Bingo. At Saturnia the *tombola* is played every night between Christmas Eve and New Year's, and if truth be told, it is probably the thing I like best about going there.

To play the *tombola*, you rent cards on which are printed twenty numbers from one to ninety. These cards have little plastic doors over them that as the numbers are called you either flip or slide down. The scoring is as follows: the first person to get two numbers on the same line calls out "*ambo*" and wins a prize; then the first person to get three numbers (*terno*); four numbers (*quaterna*); five numbers (*cinquina*); and finally the whole card (*tombola*). The calling goes on until a second person covers all his numbers, and this prize is known as the *tombolino*—the little *tombola*. At Saturnia you play not for money but things: the grand prize is a six-kilo Maremma ham.

This year, as the *tombola* begins, we settle ourselves and our cards at a green felt-covered pentagonal table. Our nearest neighbors are two elderly ladies who are playing the *tombola* simultaneously with an interminable game of gin rummy.

The calling begins. One number, two numbers. Suddenly Mark leaps up and shouts: "*Ambo!*"

Expressions of slight resentment greet this amazingly quick victory, in particular from our elderly neighbors. Mark steps up to the podium, where the master of ceremonies (actually the bartender) confirms his numbers and announces that for the *ambo*, he has won a bottle of suntan oil and a body.

"A body?" I ask as he returns, stunned, to the table.

"Yes," says one of the ladies in English. "A body is—a leotard."

The calling starts up again, and as swiftly as Mark won the *ambo* a pretty young girl who is here with her mother wins the *terno*. Her prize consists of a wild boar salami and two bodies.

"The bodies are really piling up tonight," I cannot resist saying. No one laughs.

Two numbers later Mark is leaping up again. "*Quaterna!*"

"You very lucky tonight," the bartender says to him in English, as he lists what Mark has won: a *panforte* (a Sienese sweet rather like fruitcake), another bottle of suntan oil, a book of photographs of the Maremma, and a body—"but a different body from the first one."

Another number is called. "*Cinquina!*" Mark yells.

No one shows much in the way of good tidings as the bartender recites Mark's latest round of prizes: a *pan d'oro* (another Christmas cake), a *torrone* (a Christmas candy), a jogging suit, another bottle of suntan oil, a jar of sunblock, and a bottle of dessert wine. (No body this time.)

After that, fortunately, his luck degenerates. When the *tombola* is called, the winner is an old man referred to by our neighbors only as "the engineer." Because he has won the *tombola* both last year and the year before, some corruption is suspected. Might the infamous *tangenti* that brought down the Christian Democrats have affected the innocent *tombola* too?

As for the *tombolino*, it is a tie between a gentleman in a black suit ("part of the Swiss contingent," one of the ladies remarks contemptuously) and a young girl who is here in the company of an

extremely aged man—whether her grandfather or lover no one can quite determine.

The next day—Christmas Day—we arrive early to claim our table.

"Ah, the lucky Americans," says the more loquacious of our gin-playing (and drinking) companions. "Are you going to steal our prize from us again?"

Apparently not. As the game begins, neither of us gets anywhere. *Ambo, terno, quaterna, cinquina* pass us by. (The engineer wins twice.) Then it's time for the *tombola*. Suddenly—magically—one of my cards starts filling in. "Mark!" I whisper, "I only need three numbers! Two numbers! One number! Thirty-eight!"

"*Trentotto,*" the bartender calls. "Thirty-eight."

"*Tombola!*"

I have won the ham.

"You young people are too lucky," says the Signora. "Luck should be for the old. A beautiful ham like that!" — D.L.

I came down with chicken pox on Christmas Day, at Saturnia, but the rubious pustules did not itch at first. Only the night after Christmas, when we were back in Florence, did they begin to do so, and also sting, with an exquisite and tormenting—even maddening—vengeance: I could not possibly sleep, so I finished reading a biography of Schumann ("Italy, Italy has been humming in my heart since childhood," he once wrote) and afterwards ate some walnuts our friend Pina had given us the day before.

There is no cure for chicken pox—except to scare a chicken off a fence before the sun rises—so the next morning I went to one pharmacy, and then another, to see if I might find something at least to mitigate my sufferings: there was nothing, all the pharmacists said—and all of them, once I spoke the word *varicella*, moved as far away from me as the space would physically permit: I had become, in short, a pariah.

But, perversely, there was something satisfying, to my American experience, in the way the Italians made no effort whatsoever to disguise their fear of me and my pox: I sensed their cultural memory of plague, of the great terrible thing that made a third of the world die in the fourteenth century and which provided the setup for Boccaccio's *Decameron*:

> … between March and July of the year in question [1348], what with the fury of the pestilence and the fact that so many of the sick were inadequately cared for or abandoned in their hour of need because the healthy were too terrified to approach them, it is reliably thought that [more than] a hundred thousand human lives were extinguished within the walls of the city of Florence[.]

What, finally, is the perverse satisfaction I discovered when I was as spotted as Benozzo Gozzoli's leopard? Living history—and not living in the Middle Ages. — M.M.

D.L. — Sojourning in Venice, Mary McCarthy encoun-
tered a particularly Italian parsimoniousness in the atti-
tude of her landlady toward a pet goldfish.

———————

In the kitchen reside two other candidates for
the SPCA, if there only were one in Venice: a pair
of pet goldfish in a blue-and-white china bowl. In
the bottom of the bowl is a pile of five- and ten-lire
pieces. That is all—no greenery, no algae, no scum.
The water is clear and still. The fish are extremely
pale, almost white, as though their colour had been
bled from them, and very lethargic in their move-
ments, not to say torpid. When I first looked at the
apartment, I noted the fish and supposed they would
go upstairs with the family. But when I moved in,
they were still there in the kitchen, and the signora,
drawing one of her most apologetic faces, as though
she were about to ask me for a loan of one million
lire, inquired whether they were in my way, whether
I should mind if they stayed there. I did not mind,
I said, but she must tell me what to feed them.
Nothing, declared the signora, with a droll, sidelong
look; she delights in mystifications. '*Non capisco,*' I
had to admit. '*Niente, niente!*' airily repeated the signora. They did not have to be fed; that was the principle of this aquarium. The coins generated some
sort of chemical in the water, and the fish lived on

that; she had copied the idea from a fountain in Milan. I expressed doubt. Those poor blanched creatures were dying. Certainly not, scoffed the signora; she had had them nearly two years and they were in excellent health. As a proof of this, she plunged her long forefinger with its red-painted nail into the water and tickled one fish's tail; he feebly crept away from her touch. '*Ecco!*' she said, opening her pocketbook and tossing a fresh coin into the bowl. It was a bank too, she pointed out: if I needed change for my breakfast rolls, I had only to borrow from the fish. And there was nothing to clean; between the fish and the lire, the water stayed fresh. I nodded mutely, not being fluent enough in Italian to argue further.

Left to myself in the kitchen, I have tried feeding them bread crumbs. But they refuse this nourishment, rising languidly to inspect it and them turning their heads aside like peckish invalids; if they ingest a morsel, their flaccid jaws wanly seeking a purchase on it, they at once sink, inert, to the bottom, where they lie, spent, on their silvery bed of coins. Doubtless, they are accustomed to their diet, which keeps them in a state of bare animation, between life and death. The signora does not like it if she comes down and finds the water floury from the dissolving crumbs. I watch meekly while she dumps it out and pours in fresh water; the only excuse I can give for putting her to this trouble is that the fish look so very pale. "'*Pallidi*," "*pallidi*,'" she scolds, between indignation and amusement. '*Non sono pallidi.*'

She laughs at the idea, which she finds typical of a foreigner, that a fish can turn white from hunger. And though she does not understand English or French, she knows very well that the fish are being criticized when she hears exclamations proceeding from the kitchen if I am entertaining friends. "'*Pallidi*," "*smorti*'"—we are all the same, she jests. What can I do? I am too cowardly to put the poor creatures out of their misery, which a square meal of fish food would certainly bring about. I do not wish to incur the signora's wrath; in her brusque way, she has an affection for these fish that is based on their prodigious powers of survival. So I conclude that I had best leave them as they are and take them as an allegory on Venice, a society which lived in a bowl and drew its sustenance from the filth of lucre. Once flame-colored, today it is a little pale and moribund, like the fish after two years of the signora's regimen.

Mary McCarthy, *Venice Observed* (1961)

*T*he ——— Hotel in Perugia (Goethe and
Hans Christian Andersen stayed here as
well) ... A rainy day ... "No, the National Gallery of
Umbria will not be open today" (even though there
are no college football bowl games to watch) a *cara-
biniere* tells us ... Back in the hotel ... David is work-
ing on a crossword puzzle: "Like Haydn's Surprise
Symphony ... three letters: 'i,' 'n,' blank" ... " 'g,'"
I say ... " 'ing?'" he asks ... "No, 'in g'—as in the key
of" ... On television, Zubin Mehta is conducting the
New Year's Day concert of the Vienna Philharmonic
... "*Splendida questa sala, vero?*" asks the Italian com-
mentator for the concert ... "The Austrians are not
very good-looking," I say ... "They all have yellow
skin," David says, "but that may be just the television. Brittania: 'a,' blank, blank, 'i,' 'o' 'n'" ...
"Albion," I say ... —*à propos* of England, the Philharmonic is playing a piece—Johann Strauss, Jr.'s
Russischer Marsch-Phantasie—which sounds a little
like Elgar's *Crown of India* March ... Also *à propos*
of England, a reed player in the orchestra looks like
the middle-aged E. M. Forster (whose birthday it is
today) ... Impossible not to eat some chocolate,
which we have in quantities that would have given

us considerable power in the black market in *tempo di guerra*—Perugina *Baci*, or "Kisses" (named for the Umbrian town we are in): chocolates with a crunchy hazelnut inside and the whole wrapped in a waxed paper quoting, in Italian, English, French, and Spanish, a passage from literature such as "In the confusion we stay with each other, happy to be together, without uttering a single word" (Walt Whitman) or "I will recognize her amongst thousands; she held her head in a particular way" (Thomas De Quincey) ... This whole is then wrapped in silver foil ... Austria has become, today, part of the European Economic Community (EEC): *On the Beautiful Blue Danube*, then, is as sad—the dance of a culture long lost—as the *Radetzky* March is felicitous ...

Every piece in this concert is itself, only more so ... It might be Italy ... The orchestra does not play *Roses from the South* this year, but, just the same, the flowers (or many of them) adorning the "splendid hall" are from Italy ... So reads a credit scrolled swiftly across the television screen at the end of the concert.　　　　　　　— M.M.

PODERE

A farm in Tuscany: the house, which is very old, has over the centuries lost some of its shapeliness but none of its grace. Yes, perhaps its shoulders are a bit stooped, its rear end a bit saggy; nonetheless it occupies its patch of earth with the confidence of one whose very presence has always silenced, encouraged, and redeemed. It has a roof of crumbling red and white slate, walls the color of milky coffee, many little odd-shaped windows. Its three wings, staggered and distinct, seem not so much to be built as to recline along the slope of the garden: as if in another age a girl had lain down in a meadow, her head among violets, her feet pointed toward eternity. — D.L.

GRACE

*T*he subject of Baron Wilhelm von Gloeden's photographs was unchanging: naked Sicilian boys. Roland Barthes described them as kitsch, which they are; and yet they are also sincere, which kitsch rarely is. Von Gloeden's photographs contain artifacts of the classical world, but the boys in them are neither more nor less out of place in that time than they would be in their time: they—the boys—are pan-historical. If the photographs are "about" anything, they are about the ways vision of desire is given form; about the ways that vision eludes form. After the baron took their photographs, the boys went back to being boys; no longer were they ephebes or shepherds or male Graces. They entered again into the eternal masculine. They also grew up.

— M.M.

D.L. — Henry James called the philosopher Henry Brewster, who lived most of his life in Italy, "the last of the great epistolarians." This description of Paestum comes from a letter he wrote to his lover, the composer Ethel Smyth, in 1893, and is quoted in his grandson Harry Brewster's memoir *The Cosmopolites*.

It was a splendid rush through sunlight to Sorrento and Amalfi and Paestum. Paestum hurts; it is the only place I know that would move one to tears. A desolate fever-haunted plain with wild shaggy bullocks roaming about in the brush; then lovely mountains; on the other side the sea asleep naked; and near the shore the temple of Neptune, the oldest thing in the world—impressionally at least; older than Greece and Assyria, as old as the oldest Egypt; so solemn and serene and sweet that one burns with shame; what have I done with my life? It hurts and consoles one at once.

Henry Brewster, letter to Ethel Smyth (1893)

*T*oward the end of the fourteenth century, the British mercenary Sir John Hawkwood—having defended the Florentine Republic against its enemies—asked that an equestrian statue be erected in his honor. Typically, the Florentines responded by commissioning not a statue, but a *trompe l'oeil* fresco of a statue, to be painted by Paolo Uccello on the north wall of the Duomo. Expediency might have been the motive, or cheapness (this was Florence, after all), or some distaste for excessive honorifics; but I think more likely the Florentines simply liked the idea of scoring off Sir John—as well as the generations of visitors who would be "taken in" by the illusion.

In the Baroque Church of San Ignazio, in Rome, the magnificent dome is in fact a fresco painted by Andrea Pozzo on flat canvas. The illusion is so convincing that an American lady, taken there recently by a friend of ours, refused absolutely to accept it. Likewise in Sestri Levante half the stonemasonry on the outsides of the buildings is *trompe l'oeil*. Water drips from a pot of flowers, a cat licks itself on a ledge, the ledge casts a shadow; but everything—water, flowers, cat, ledge, *and* shadow—

is painted. The bricks are painted, as are the weeds growing between the bricks. Even the street signs at the corner of Via Portobello and the Salita alla Penisola di Levante are illusory.

A candy shop in Milan displays in its windows strawberries, figs, melons, oranges, apples, bananas, and kiwis—all false, shaped from marzipan; hamburgers of marzipan on marzipan buns; bowls of marzipan pasta topped with marzipan *ragù* and grated marzipan (a near anagram for parmesan) cheese. And what is *trippa alla fiorentina*, after all— that dish of tripe sliced into noodle lengths and served with tomato sauce and grated cheese—but a grotesque parody of pasta?

The delight Italians take in things that appear to be other than themselves is double: yes, the playing of a trick (*trucco*, which also means makeup) gives the trickster a naughty *frisson;* but I also think that the old Renaissance notion of *virtù*—of dazzlement—is reinvoked every time a Ligurian housepainter finishes off his job with a false flowerpot. In this spirit Mantegna created his famous Christ with the foreshortened feet, Tiepolo his dizzying ceilings. Art historians these days often bemoan the paucity of contemporary Italian artists, declaring Italy a museum culture, a mausoleum for past glories; and

yet isn't it possible that the old cleverness and curiosity and wit that sparked the Renaissance have
persevered, albeit in the realm of the so-called "com-
mercial" arts? True, a baker who works in marzipan
is no Mantegna—but doesn't some of Mantegna's
wizardry, his *sprezzatura*, linger still in fingers that
forge from almond paste such lean and fanciful
illusions?

Finally, living in Italy encourages the impulse to
create illusions. Mark has felt it on occasion, once
going so far as to invent an eggless version of
spaghetti alla carbonara—a *trompe la langue* rendi-
tion—the recipe for which I offer here on behalf
both of the curious and those who cannot eat eggs.

Italian Pleasures

Mock Spaghetti alla Carbonara

Chop a white onion and fry it in some good olive oil along with a few leaves of sage. To this mixture add one can of white *cannellini* beans. Let the whole cook for about five minutes, then add an envelope of powdered saffron, stirring until the whole has the consistency of beaten egg yolks. Put the mixture in a food processor and process briefly until smooth. Meanwhile fry some chopped *pancetta* or bacon with black pepper. While the spaghetti is cooking put the "eggs" in a bowl and mix into them some grated pecorino and parmesan cheese. When the spaghetti is done, toss with the "eggs" and the *pancetta*, adding a bit of the cooking water from the pasta pot if needed. — D.L.

D.L. — When I moved to Italy I expected the country to be a lot of things; I never expected it to be boring. Yet Italian boredom can be an exquisite delicacy. A dissolute aristocrat sums up the matter for Lord Byron in Frederic Prokosch's novel *The Missolonghi Manuscript*.

"The Italians are adorable but *au fond* they lack mystery. Life is exquisite in Italy but in the end atrociously boring. The French are occasionally nasty but at least they have depth. The Italians live on the surface. Their life is in the piazza. They feel passions, *bien sûr*, but they are the passions of the opera, full of gestures and grimaces, accompanied by a fine melodious resonance."

Frederic Prokosch, *The Missolonghi Manuscript* (1968)

*M*y friend Beppe—a cook—represents all that can be best about Italians. Because he worries that the sun will die in fifty million years, he is a man in the tradition of Galileo. Beppe's older brother shares the modern Italian's sad and inordinate fascination with gadgetry: possessor of four watches within the last year, each more ramified than the one before. He is the sort of person who would buy the condom invented by Lino Missio, a Genovese, that, thanks to a microchip, plays *"un brano di Beethoven"* if it breaks. Beppe's watch, on the other hand, gives only the hour (and, doubtless, his condoms are not musical). It is by instinct that he makes a perfect *spaghetti alla carbonara*, yellow as the troublesome sun of the Florentine Galileo. — M.M.

A snide but useful list of "Don'ts" in the English section of the weekly magazine *Roma C'è* includes the advice: "Don't be afraid to drink the water on the street." Roman water is praised not only for its taste but for the quantities of calcium it contains: wonderful for the bones and pizza crusts, and terrible for showerheads and dishwashers (the insides of which will calcify if you don't treat them monthly with rock salt). In the street water pours perpetually from the mouths of fish or what are called in art history "allegorical figures" or a marble wine barrel held by a marble dwarf or brass spigots with little holes on the top like the spout holes of whales. If you want to take a drink you plug up the stream that runs perpetually from the spigot's mouth with your forefinger, thus causing the water to arc through the hole.

On sweltering summer days, no water tastes better to me than the water on the streets of Rome. I don't envy the tourists clutching their little bottles of mineral water—Panna or San Pellegrino or for those who believe that anything French is better than anything Italian, Evian. How can water from a bottle taste better than a fresh running stream? Old

Roman ladies who would never go out even on the hottest summer day without their pearls carry little plastic folding cups in their purses, and during a break in the *Roma Nascosta*, or "Hidden Rome," historical tours, stand gratefully around the fountains in their mint green silk pantsuits, drinking the water that pours from a Renaissance *putto*'s lips. It is like the water at the end of Elizabeth Bishop's wonderful poem "At the Fishhouses,"

> drawn from the cold hard mouth
> of the world, derived from the rocky breasts
> forever, flowing and drawn, and since
> our knowledge is historical, flowing, and flown.

the same water with which Nero filled arenas to stage mock sea battles.

Perhaps Rome, and not Venice, is really the city of water. — D.L.

M.M. — A few weeks after I read Carlo Levi's *Christ Stopped at Eboli*, I met a boy from Basilicata—the region of Italy where the memoir takes place. When I mentioned to him that I had read it, he smiled, told me that his grandfather had known Levi and was in the book (Don Cosimino, the postmaster). Italy is a small country.

———————

It was the only toilet in the village, and probably there was not another one within a radius of fifty miles. In the houses of the well-to-do there were still ancient seats of monumental proportions in carved wood, miniature thrones with an air of authority about them. I was told, although I never saw them with my own eyes, that there existed pairs of matrimonial seats, side by side, for couples so devoted that they could not endure even the briefest separation. The poor, of course had nothing, and this lack made for strange customs. In Grassano, at almost regular hours, in the early morning and again in the evening, windows were surreptitiously opened and the wrinkled hands of old women were to be seen emptying the contents of chamber pots into the street. These were 'black magic' or bad luck hours. In Gagliano the ceremony was neither as widespread nor as regular; so precious a fertilizer for the fields could not be wasted.

The complete absence of this simple apparatus in the region created almost ineradicable habits, which, entwined with other familiar ways of doing things, came to posses an almost poetic and sentimental character. Lasala, the carpenter, an alert 'American', who had been mayor of Grassano many years before and who kept in the depths of the enormous radio-gramophone he had brought back with him from New York—along with recordings of Caruso and of the arrival of the transatlantic flier, De Pinedo, in America—some speeches commemorating the murdered Matteotti, told me this story. A group of immigrants from Grassano used to meet every Sunday for an outing to the country after their hard week's work in New York …

'There were eight or ten of us: a doctor, a druggist, some tradesmen, a hotel waiter, and a few workers, all of us from the same town and acquainted with each other since we were children. Life is depressing there among the skyscrapers, where there's every possible convenience, elevators, revolving doors, subways, endless streets and buildings, but never a bit of green earth. Homesickness used to get the better of us. On Sundays we took a train for miles and miles in search of some open country.

When finally we reached a deserted spot, we were all as happy as if a great weight had been lifted from our shoulders. And beneath a tree, all of us together would let down our trousers . . . What joy! We could feel the fresh air and all of nature around us. It wasn't like those American toilets, shiny and all alike. We felt like boys again, as if we were back in Grassano; we were happy, we laughed and we breathed for a moment the air of home. And when we had finished we shouted together: *"Viva l'Italia!"* The words came straight from our hearts.'

Carlo Levi, *Christ Stopped at Eboli* (1945)

A friend of mine who lived many years in Paris recounts an argument between a Frenchman and an Italian in which the Frenchman asserted that Italian cuisine did not exist. Why? Because the staples of Italian cooking were tomatoes from the New World, corn from the New World, coffee from the New World, and pasta from China. "Hell, if it wasn't for tomatoes, corn, coffee, and pasta, there wouldn't even *be* Italian cooking!" To which the Italian replied: "No, there wouldn't. We'd have to eat French food."

The Frenchman was right about the tomatoes and coffee. (It is hard to imagine an Italy without tomato sauce and cappuccino, but that Italy existed far longer than the one we know.) Pasta is a different matter. Until recently, it was assumed that pasta had been brought from the Orient by Marco Polo, along with tea. Then historians unearthed a series of documents attesting to the production and exportation of pasta in Italy as early as A.D. 1154. Immediately the Italian pasta factories started trumpeting these documents; a whole museum was built around them, the Museo Spaghetti on Piazza Scanderbeg in Rome. "We invented this," the museum

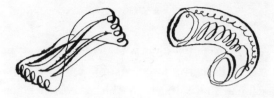

declared, proud to be able to take credit for at least one thing for which Italy was already famous. (Meanwhile the pasta authority Massimo Alberini, in the magazine *Pasta & C.*, exposed the source of the original libel: an American trade publication called *The Macaroni Journal* that in 1929 published an article titled "A Saga of Cathay.") Still, even without the documents I doubt most Italians would worry whether they invented pasta: what matters to them— what they take pride in—is that they *perfected* pasta.

And what perfection! What variety! Not only of shapes, but of names, which also vary from region to region. One man's *linguine* is another man's *bavette*. What Southerners call *vermicelli* Northerners call *spaghettini*. Then there are the innumerable fresh pastas: Tuscan *pici*, made without egg and rolled, play-dough style, between the palms; all manner of stuffed pastas—*tortellini* and *cappelletti* and *agnolotti* and Sardinian *seadas*, filled with sweet cheese and fried. In the Marche, I have eaten *tagliatelle* made only with the white of an egg, or with a

flour prepared from dried fava beans; in Liguria, *corzetti*—circles of pasta stamped to look like medallions—and *trofie*, little nubby-ended twists tossed with *pesto*, potatoes, and green beans.

As with so many other things, Italians are very set in their ways about pasta. Pater's dictum "Failure is forming habits" would not go over well here. In most Italian households it is the usual spaghetti or penne that prevail, though curiously a recent survey revealed that while Southern Italians prefer their penne to be *lisce*—without ridges—Northern Italians like theirs *rigate*—with ridges.

When Italian pasta companies attempt to modernize or improve upon tradition, a stubborn resistance tends to take hold. In 1987, Barilla introduced, with great fanfare, two new shapes designed by a firm of architects: *bifure*, bifurcated rectangles, and *trifoglie*, three-pronged spaghetti. For a while much fuss was made over these new shapes, but in the end most Italians went back to their usual penne and spaghetti, and today the "exclusive shapes of the architects" are almost as hard to find as a can of New Coke.

Barilla continues to think up new forms—usually with the same results. Indeed, when we first came here, caught up in the enthusiasm that the pasta aisle at an Italian supermarket can inspire, we bought a box of mushroom-shaped *nicchiole*. Two years later, they're still in the cabinet.

These days even the famed De Cecco pasta company of Fara S. Martino (Abruzzo)—long a bastion of the traditional—can't seem to resist getting in on the innovation act. They have recently started marketing *racchettine*—little tennis rackets—a shape that adds a whole new dimension to the expression "Dinner is served."   — D.L.

FLAVOR

*S*apore di mare, sapore di sale ("flavor of the sea, flavor of salt"), a famous Italian song runs. (And it is true that in Italy salt—most of it from Sicily—is saltier than anywhere in the world.) Things taste like themselves here in a way that they do less and less in America, where rational thinking gives us the seedless (and bland) tomato, or a patented garlic that does not scent the breath. Such intentions seem bizarre to Italians, for whom garlic that does not scent the breath simply isn't garlic.*

Flavor is what I miss whenever I leave Italy and what I seek as soon as I come back. It is a hard thing to describe; still, when something tastes the way it ought to, you recognize it instantly—authenticity always being a self-defining experience. Arugula and olive oil, cherries and figs, *prosciutto di Parma* sliced into transparent sheets, then draped over a wedge of melon: such foods announce themselves quietly, with assurance; then, just as quietly, they amaze

---

* Since writing this piece, I have been alarmed to see numerous advertisements on the sides of Roman buses for just such garlic; whether it will be a success or go the way of *bifure*, however, remains to be seen.

the tongue. Even the Italian flag pays homage to this principle, for what do the red, green, and white stripes represent, if not tomato, basil, and mozzarella? — D.L.

M.M. — Norman Douglas lived much of his life in Italy, and wrote a novel titled *South Wind* that takes place in Capri. The story of Fra Egidio included here is an homage to a friend of ours from that region; a friend who, before we had read Douglas's book, told us other stories of Calabrian animals—those of Martino, a lamb, and Antonella, a trout, the loveliest among them.

Thus a cow belonging to Fra Egidio's monastery was once stolen by an impious butcher, and cut up into the usual joints with a view to a clandestine sale of the meat. The saint discovered the beast's remains, ordered that they should be laid together on the floor in the shape of a living cow, with the entrails, head and so forth in their natural positions; then, having made the sign of the cross with his cord upon the slaughtered beast, and rousing up all his faith, he said: "In the name of God and of Saint Pasquale, arise, Catherine!" (Catherine was the cow's name.) "At these words the animal lowed, shook itself, and stood up on its feet alive, whole and strong, even as it had been before it was killed."

Norman Douglas, *Old Calabria* (1915)

Ragù—meat sauce for pasta—is as close to a national dish as Italy has to offer. Like most things Italian, however, *ragùs* vary from region to region. The type that comes close to being a *ragù franca* is probably the Bolognese variety. It is not complicated to prepare. To a *soffritto* of onions, carrot, and celery (never garlic) cooked in a mixture of olive oil and butter you add a comparatively small amount of ground meat: usually a mix of beef, pork, sausage, and *pancetta*. The whole is then simmered, first in milk, then in meat broth, then in red wine. Finally tomato paste or purée is added and the *ragù* left to steep and thicken. A Bolognese *ragù* is always served over fresh *tagliatelle:* never dried penne or spaghetti. But Bologna is hardly the end of the *ragù* story.

In Abruzzo, where sheep are raised, the traditional *ragù* is made with lamb, chunks of sweet red pepper, and rosemary. To the Tuscan variety, which sometimes omits tomato, peas or ham, and even lemon juice are added; the meat can be rabbit, hare, or wild boar. According to Elizabeth Romer in *The Tuscan Year,* an Umbrian *ragù* is distinguished from its Tuscan cousin by the addition of butter, dried mushrooms, chicken giblets, and heavy cream. A lady we know from Cosenza adds cloves. Of course, even within regions, recipes vary from kitchen to kitchen.

Another important point in the *polemica* about meat sauce: how to distinguish a *ragù* from a *sugo*. In his *Grande Libro della Cucina Toscana* Paolo Petroni lists the following differences: 1. In a *sugo* the meat is cut into small pieces; in a *ragù* it is ground. 2. In a *sugo* the *odori* (onion, celery, carrot) are cooked first before the meat is put into the pan; in a *ragù* the *odori* and the meat are cooked together. 3. To a *ragù*, you add broth and wine; to a *sugo* neither. 4. You would never add butter, cream, or milk to a *sugo*, whereas you can do so to a *ragù*. (Warning: Signore Petroni lists these rules with authority, as if they were written by God. But they are not universal, and as caviling over unimportant things is one of the greatest of Italian pleasures, a public reading of Petroni's laws would probably soon lead to riot.)

Which brings us, finally, to that anemic red sauce my mother used to buy in jars when I was a child (Ragù brand). How do we reconcile that stuff with the many variations of *ragù* found in Italy? Just another American bastardization? No, in fact. Instead, like most Italo-American foods, Ragù brand spaghetti sauce has its origins in the Neapolitan recipes that the first immigrants brought with them when they crossed the Atlantic. As Martino Ragusa has written in an article in the April 1994 issue of *Sale e Pepe*, "The Two Homelands of the *Ragù*," Neapolitan *ragù* is another kettle of sauce altogether.

Martino Ragusa strikes me as a writer to be trusted. He is photographed on the first page of his article in a neon blue shirt, purple pants, and hiking boots, recumbent upon a stack of fresh tomatoes. To make a Neapolitan *ragù*, he explains—and with his name, he must know what he's talking about—you first cook some chopped white onion in olive oil over a low flame until it caramelizes. Into the pot of onion you then throw one or two pork chops and a large piece of pork loin, let the meat brown, add salt and pepper, and finally pour in a glass of white wine. You then put into the pot a good quantity of tomato *conserva*, ideally homemade. And then—this is the fun part—you let the sauce bubble (*pippiare*) for five hours. Five hours, taking care that it never boils, which would be ruin; five hours, giving an occasional stir, watching, dozing: a "ritual of concentration," Ragusa calls it, almost a form of Zen meditation for which the simmering sauce functions as the mantra. Five hours. No wonder Italians say *ragù* is a dish only the *portiere* or concierge has time to prepare.

(As George Eliot observed, "Time, like money, is measured by our needs.")

When the five hours are up, you take out the meat, which is served as the second course. The meat-infused tomato sauce you pour over dried pasta—spaghetti or rigatoni—and "pass" (as old Italian-American cookbooks phrase it) with grated fresh pecorino.

Postscript: In no Italian shop have I once seen a package of that immemorial pasta known in America as *ziti*. Yes, De Cecco packages ziti, but only for sale outside of Italy. In Naples, on the other hand, there is a pasta known as *zite:* big hollow tubes, as long as spaghetti and as thick as penne. When Ronzoni and other American pasta companies describe their pasta as "ziti" (cut), it is probably the old Neapolitan grandfather to which they are referring. No doubt the American *zito* is a Neapolitan *zita* sliced into bite-size chunks that can be forked more neatly: yet another act of deference to New World notions of gustatory *gentilezza*. — D.L.

he best guidebook to Rome is Georgina Masson's *The Companion Guide to Rome*, first published in 1965. Though the bus numbers have changed since then, and the *Monte Testaccio* is now closed to the public—this potsherd, composed of fragments of *amphorae*, was forty-five meters high when Masson wrote, but is now only thirty-six meters high—the book is still something of a bible. Ideally, the traveler to Rome keeps two guides: Masson's, and a newer one to correct the anachronisms.

It was with Masson as my companion that I ventured to the Trappist Monastery of the Three Fountains. St. Paul was martyred here, some say, and the fountains gushed in the three places where his head bounced when it was cut off. There is nothing speculative about the beautiful mosaic of the four seasons from Ostia Antica in the church of S. Paolo alle Tre Fontane, however; nothing speculative about the chocolate—milk chocolate and dark chocolate and chocolate with hazelnuts—made by the Trappist monks and on sale in their little shop. Alas, the *Aceto Galenico* once made by the monks— "a sovereign remedy," Masson writes, "to anyone who lives in Rome and suffers from headaches when the scirocco blows"—is no longer to be found.

From the monastery, I took a taxi to the Marconi *Metropolitana* stop, and thence to our apartment in the quarter of, and with a view of part of, the Colosseum. On my return, a proud couple stepped onto the train at Garbatella: she with a violin, and he with a *"preghiera,"* a prayer, for their oldest daughter—who, because she was becoming blind, had had to leave the university. On my way to the church in the morning, a filthy, grasping gypsy girl had begged futilely on the *Metropolitana*, but when this mother began to play *"Santa Lucia,"* every woman's pocketbook flew open with an offering.

The bouncing head of St. Paul or the dimmed sight of a Roman girl: Italians believe what they choose. — M.M.

*W*e have a friend from Milan who now lives in New York. ("To be a *borghese* from Milan is the greatest thing in Italy," she says, "and the worst thing in the world.") The first evening I spent at her house was one of the happiest I have known: she and her husband made a shrimp and asparagus risotto and a simple salad, then we played *Scopa* (an addictive Italian card game) and ate ice cream and Pepperidge Farm "Mint Milano" cookies (of course). The next morning Giovanna, who was then pregnant, came downstairs into the kitchen, and said, "Coff-ee. I am destroyed. I must have coff-ee." I drank the dark and vital stuff with her, and ate a few more Mint Milano cookies, and thus did I come to love Italian coffee—and coffee with Italians.

In fact, coffee is my day's incipient pleasure, not least because it takes me into the world. Most everyone has a favorite bar or *pasticceria*—mine, in Florence, is Robiglio, of which there are three branches. My Robiglio (the one on Via dei Servi) is decorated in a somewhat 1960s style, and so is one of the women who work behind the pastry counter: she paints her eyes to look like Elizabeth Taylor's in

Cleopatra. Robiglio has superb sweet things—a *budino di riso*, a *pasta della nonna* ("grandmother's tart," with custard and peach and almonds)—but its *ragione di esistere*, for me, is its coffee. Illy Caffe was the brand used until fairly recently (Sig. Illy is the mayor of Trieste), but no matter the brand, the secret of a great cappuccino is the way the milk is poured. Marco Zani and Marco Altieri—the two barmen, or *baristi*—have been initiated into that mystery.

There is a false idea in America that cappuccino is an all-day drink. But, in fact, the six modes of cappuccino (so named because its color resembles that of a Capuchin monk's habit) belong, for the most part, to the morning: Italians would not drink a cappuccino after supper. *Then*, the Italian thing is a small and potent *caffè espresso* ("Mother of neurasthenia," as Norman Douglas called it), of which there are endless variations: *macchiato* (with milk—either hot or cold), *macchiato senza schiuma* (without foam), *basso*, *corretto* (with liquor), *lungo*, and *ristretto*.

A good coffee is defined, according to Florentines, by three S's: *scuro*, *scottante*, and *scroccato*—dark, hot, and paid for by someone else. (Thoreau writes, "beware of all enterprises that require new clothes"; likewise, beware of all places that require payment—the scurrilous *scontrino*—before the coffee is drunk.)

And, as a *principessa* tells us, coffee tastes better on a rainy day. (Speaking of rain: one autumn the Arno, swollen into turbulence and awesomeness, ran the color of cappuccino.)   — M.M.

*O*ur first summer here, I had a very hard time figuring out how to order an iced cappuccino. The first few times I simply asked for a *cappuccino freddo* or *caffè freddo*. (A mistake: usually I ended up being served a cappuccino made with cold milk— *cappuccino tiepido*, a lukewarm mess.) Then a friend told me that the correct term for iced coffee in an Italian bar is *caffè shakerato*.

Like most Italian processes, the preparation of a *caffè shakerato* is not without its elements of ritual. First the barman takes a cocktail glass or martini glass and, inserting it facedown into his ice bucket, gives it a few twirls to cool it. Next he prepares an *espresso* in the customary tiny cup. Next he takes a gleaming stainless-steel cocktail shaker (preferably Alessi), fills it with ice, pours in the *espresso*, adds cold milk and a little sugar, and finally with some embarrassment lifts the shaker above his head and—well—shakes it, hard, as if to the rhythm of a samba, until the loud ruckus of the ice cubes diminishes into the faintest castanet clack. Then he removes the top from the shaker and strains the chilled, hazelnut-colored liquid into the waiting glass. There is always exactly enough to fill it up.

It takes only twenty seconds or so to drink down a *caffe shakerato*—but what cold ecstasy!   — D.L.

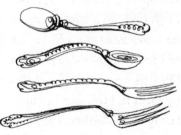

M.M. — I spoke only opera Italian when we settled in Italy, and this was, as Bernard Levin observes, of little practical help. We arrived in July, and so I had to wait six months before I could work *"che gelida manina"* into a conversation.

———————

The first time I ever went to Florence I arrived badly in need of a haircut. The morning after my arrival, therefore, I set forth in search of one, only to realize that I did not know the Italian for a hairdresser. However, though I might not be able to speak Rossini's language, at least I know what his best-known opera was called. I approached a policeman; but I paused. To ask for *'un barbiere'* would be simple; but I calculated that a Florentine policeman's pay would hardly run to more than a modest establishment in a back street, where they would probably cut my ears off. How was I to make known that I wanted a high-class barber, a de luxe barber, a veritable Figaro among barbers? Then I recollected what Figaro, in the *Largo al factotum*, actually calls himself: he insists that he leads the life *'D'un barbiere—di qualità, di qualità.'*

I got my barber of quality, and my haircut, and the episode set me wondering just how far round Europe an opera-loving traveller could get, using nothing but the Italian, German and French that he knew from the operatic stage. Even a moderately assiduous opera-goer would have at his disposal a wide variety of ways in which to swear undying love to ladies, or to announce that he has just been fatally stabbed, shot or poisoned. The briefest study of *Die Walküre* will tell you what to do should you happen to fall in love with your long-lost sister, and from *Siegfried* you may learn the proper etiquette for conducting an affair with your aunt. And from the last scene of *Falstaff* you can learn, as the fat man tells the chimes of midnight, how to count in Italian from one to twelve. But all that would still leave some crucial gaps. Nobody in opera buys a railway ticket or a pair of shoes, let alone a ticket for the opera; nobody asks the way to the Town Hall, the nearest bus-stop or the lavatory; nobody books a room at a hotel; nobody tries to explain to a policeman why he has parked his car where no car may be parked; indeed, I know of only one opera in which anybody is even offered a normal drink, and in that, *Madam Butterfly*, the choice that Pinkerton offers Sharpless is restricted to milk-punch, whatever that might be, and whisky.

Bernard Levin, *Conducted Tour* (1981)

*O*ne of the stories of my parents' courtship is this: they were together in a record store in Tallahassee, and stopped to browse over a new recording of old Southern songs. The cover of the album pictured an antebellum mansion surrounded by grand, mossy oaks, and this prompted my dad to say, "That reminds me of home." My mother's heart leapt—then my dad added drily, "We have moss, too."

The acanthus-topped columns of the old Southern mansions are weighty with romance and sadness for those who come from that place. Acanthus is not native to the South, and for this reason its use as an architectural motif conferred unique mystery upon it (as upon the mandrake). Acanthus is native to Rome, however: near the Colosseum, in hot midsummer, I saw it for the first time—a thing familiar, intimidating. By what dispensation could the leaves that adorned ruined marble columns in Mississippi flourish with such botanical alacrity in the shadow of other ruins?

All I know is that at the beginning of the July week we settled in Rome, B. B. King (also from Mississippi) played here: where there is acanthus— the shrub of ruin—the Blues are at home.   — M.M.

*A*lthough Paris is the European city most renowned for its cafés, it is in Roman cafés—particularly those clustering the Piazza Navona—that I have most often felt that famous café feeling: the desire to stretch out one's legs, pull a notebook from a satchel, and write.

It was at an outdoor table at the Café Colonna on the Piazza Navona that in 1982 I wrote the first draft of a short story called "Viewing Pleasure" (as in "For Your"); later, it became "Danny in Transit," and appeared in my collection, *Family Dancing*. I remember devoting whole hot July afternoons to that story, all the while nursing a Coca-Cola into which a wedge of lemon slowly leaked its juice. (Having little money, I made each Coca-Cola last several hours.) Across the way the water from Bernini's famous baroque fountain of the Four River Gods cooled the air a little. And when I lifted my head it was the eponymous protaganists of that fountain that I saw, their faces filled with repulsion as they looked upon the ugly church Bernini's rival Borromeo had erected on the other side of the square. (Upon the fountain's completion, an insulted Borromeo installed a disdainful angel on the roof.)

Fortune tellers and caricaturists cluttered the piazza
with their little makeshift stalls. I don't know why,
but something about this very Roman scene called
up New Jersey summers in my imagination, swim-
ming pools and barbecues and childhood griefs. (An
American never feels more American than when he
is abroad.) So I wrote and wrote, until the setting
sun prickled my burned arms, at which point I would
put away my notebook and head back to my tiny
hotel room (it was only big enough to hold a single
bed and a sink), and after a lonely dinner, crouch
away another couple of hours, writing in the most
ungainly of postures. How innocent I was in those

days—innocent of ambition, of desire, of comfort! I hardly ever thought, "I want this," "I need that." Instead I looked, and covered sheets with words.

Now, thirty-four, and burdened with that self-consciousness that must perhaps inevitably come with age (not to mention the bad posture that is the inevitable consequence of a youth spent crouched over notepads), I live in Rome and sit sometimes in that same café. Of course I don't need to budget the price of a Coke anymore. Still, hunched over in one of those uncomfortable little lawn chairs, notepad in hand, something of the self to whom the last ten years didn't happen revives. My mother is not dead, I have not had to endure the pleasures and vagaries of success, I have never owned a house or been sued. In another Roman time nymphs turned routinely into trees, men changed into women, drops of gore from a wound in a warrior's side fell to the ground as tiny flowers. The world is less pliable today; yet I am convinced that what little of that old transformative power remains lingers in the Roman piazzas.

— D.L.

M.M. — Jocelyn Brooke, English writer and amateur botanist (among his works is an exhaustive study of the English orchid), tells in a memoir titled *The Dog at Clambercrown* of a trip he made to Sicily. The story of Demeter and Persephone was, since his boyhood, Brooke's favorite myth ("my first introduction to the agonies of homesickness"). He went from Enna to Pergusa, the "home" of Persephone, on Easter Sunday.

───────

Here, more than ever, one was haunted by a sense of some ancient, immitigable tragedy; more even than the hills of Santa Panagia, or the mountain hideout of the *capo di Mafia*, did this landscape breathe an air of deadness and desolation; here, at the 'navel of Sicily', the whole dark and vengeful spirit of the island seemed gathered into a central nucleus of potential terror and violence. Nothing, certainly, could have been more at odds with the northern-European, 'literary' concept of Enna, with its 'fair fields', its lilies and roses and all the joys of the resurgent spring; yet the Greeks, I thought, had been right: for here—and here only—that most ancient and most potent of myths must surely have had its birth; here among these sad fields and desolate hillsides which, on this bleak spring evening of the mid-twentieth century, seemed to be awaiting, with an age-old and undiminished expectancy, the renewal of the miracle—the rebirth of the Corn-goddess from the dark womb of winter.

———————

Jocelyn Brooke, *The Dog at Clambercrown* (1955)

One of the most exciting moments of my life was lining up on the Via della Pergola, in Florence, to buy tickets for a recital by the pianist Sviatoslav Richter—a recital that he would end with a work from the second of his albums that I bought and listened to in Lantana, Florida, when I was half my present age: Schubert's *Wanderer* fantasy.

The first of his records I bought was *Richter in Italy*. I never imagined that I would hear its title.

— M.M.

*T*hat first summer we used to sit out on the
terrace on warm July evenings, woozy from
the fumes of the citronella candles, watching the
movies that were projected every night at the Forte
di Belvedere. This was difficult: the Belvedere was
half a mile away, across the river, so that from our
terrace the screen on its hill seemed the size of a
Post-It note, flickering with color. Still, when it was
very quiet, or the breeze was blowing just so, we
could make out the voices of the actors (dubbed, of
course), and guess which movie was being shown.

Later, in Rome, we discovered the park of the
Colle Oppio. Here, amid the ruins of Trajan's Baths,
movies are projected one after the other late into the
hot July night. *Moglie mia*, a Roman saying goes, *in
agosto, non ti conosco;* "dear wife, in August I don't

know you." What else is there to do but go to the movies? Young couples drifted in and out of the makeshift theater, stopping perhaps to have a *grattachecca*—shaved ice flavored with lemon and coconut—or browse at the remaindered book stall, where gigantic illustrated editions of *The Divine Comedy* could be purchased at half price. For me, the most dramatic presence at the Colle Oppio wasn't the screen, however, or the raw remains of Trajan's Baths, but the Colosseum itself, bathed in a golden light, both looming and luminous beyond the park. As once Romans crowded through its eighty-eight *cunei* to see gladiators fight gladiators, or slaughter elephants or zebras or rhinos, now Romans perched on plastic chairs and watched Audrey Hepburn (dubbed, of course) thrusting her hand into the open *bocca della verità*. If you tell a lie, they say it will bite it off. A gentler entertainment? Times have changed in the eternal city—but not so much.   — D.L.

ickets to out-of-town concerts in Italy are difficult to come by because no system exists for ordering them over the telephone. When the pianist Evgeny Kissin gave a recital in Bologna, however, my friend Cosimo managed to charm the woman in the box office of the Teatro Communale: she said that she would hold a ticket for me if I would promise to get to Bologna *subito*.

I did so—*per fortuna* the trains were running—and just after 9:00 P.M. I was seated as Kissin walked from the wings and played Schubert and Chopin, Schumann and Liszt. This was his formal program, but in the end it was only a prelude: he was so well-loved by the Bolognese, who recalled him to the stage some forty times, that he played thirteen encores*—the last, Liszt's *Harmonies du soir*, about

---

* Liszt, *Waldesrauschen*; Chopin, *Grande-Valse* in A-flat; Schubert-Tausig, *Marche-militaire*; Chopin, mazurka in F minor, op. 68; Chopin, waltz in E minor, op. post.; Bach-Kempff, *Siciliano*; Tchaikovský, "Nata-Valse"; Rachmaninov, prelude, op. 23, no. 2; Schubert, sonata in A minor, op. 143 (third movement); Schubert, sonata in B major, op. 147 (second movement); Liszt, *La leggierezza*; Liszt, *Transcendental Etude* no. 10; Liszt, *Harmonies du soir*.

12:30 A.M. The audience, conscious that it was witnessing—as well as bringing about—musical history, called "*grazie*" ("thanks")—not "*bis*" ("encore")—each time Kissin returned to the stage.

A few months later in Florence, when he performed the Rachmaninov third concerto, I sent a note to Kissin asking him if he had ever played so many encores as he did in Bologna. "I only prepared three encores," he wrote; "the rest I was just playing from the memory. I had no other concert like that in my life—but, I think, it's worth being a musician just for one such concert."

I think it's worth being a concert-goer just for one such concert.   — M.M.

M.M. — The theater is a vital part of Italian life—even if ordinary Italian life is apt to be theatrical. *The Leopard* is the most famous of Giuseppe Tomasi di Lampedusa's few works, but "Places in my Infancy," in which he recollects the theater in his family's house, is the one for which I have the greatest affection because much of my own happiness has been discovered in Italian theaters.

The best of it was that this theatre (which of course also had a public entrance from the piazza) was often used.

Every now and again a company of actors would arrive: these were strolling players who, generally in summer, moved on carts from one village to the other, staying two or three days in each to give performances. In Santa Margherita where there was a proper theatre they stayed longer, two or three weeks.

At ten in the morning the leading actor would call in frock-coat and top hat to ask for permission to perform in the theatre; he would be received by my father or, in his absence, by my mother, who of course gave permission, refused any rent (or rather made a contract for a token rental of fifty *centesimi* for the two weeks), and also paid a subscription for our own box. After which the leading actor left, to return half-an-hour later and request a loan of furniture. These companies travelled, in fact, with a few bits of painted scenery but no stage furniture, which would have been too costly and inconvenient to carry about. The furniture was granted, and in the evening we would recognise our armchairs, tables and wardrobes on the stage (they were not our best, I'm sorry to say). They were handed back punctually at the moment of departure, sometimes so garishly revarnished that we had to ask other companies to desist from this well-intentioned practice. Once, if I remember right, the leading lady also called on us, a fat good-natured Ferrarese of about thirty who was to play *La Dame aux Camélias* for the closing night. Finding her own wardrobe unsuitable for the solemnity of the occasion she came to ask my mother for an evening dress: and so the Lady of the Camellias appeared in a very low-cut robe of Nile green covered in silver spangles.

These companies wandering round country villages have now vanished, which is a pity. The scenery was primitive, the acting obviously bad; but they played with gusto and fire and their "presence" was certainly more life-like than are the pallid shades of fifth-rate films now shown in the same villages.

Every night there was a play, and the repertoire was most extensive; the whole of nineteenth-century drama passed on that stage: Scribe, Rovetta, Sardou, Giacometti and Torelli. Once there was even a *Hamlet*, the first time in fact that I ever heard it. And the audience, partly of peasants, were attentive and warm in their applause. At Santa Margherita, at least, these companies did good business, with theatre and furniture free and their draught-horses put up and foddered in our stables.

I used to attend every night, except on one night of the season called "black night", when some French *pochade*, reputed indecent, was shown. Next day our local friends came to report on this libertine performance, and were usually very disappointed as they had expected something much more salacious.

I enjoyed it all enormously, and so did my parents. The better companies at the end of their season were offered a kind of rustic garden party with a simple but abundant buffet out in the garden, which cheered up the stomachs, often empty I fear, of those excellent strolling players.

But already in the last year in which I spent a long period at Santa Margherita, 1921, companies of actors no longer came, and instead flickering films were shown. The war had killed off, among others, these poor and picturesque wandering companies which had their own artistic merits and were, I have an idea, the training school of many a great Italian actor and actress of the nineteenth century, Duse among others.

———————————

Giuseppe Tomasi di Lampedusa, "Places in my Infancy" (1961)

ASHES

*L*ate in September of 1994 Reginald and Margaret Green of Bodega Bay, California, lost their seven-year-old son Nicholas while driving along the coastal highway from Salerno to Calabria. They were sitting in the front seat of their rented car, and Nicholas and his sister were sleeping in the back. Being tourists (and not speaking Italian) the Greens didn't know that this particular stretch of highway is notorious for banditry. Likewise, they didn't understand why a car pulled up alongside theirs; or what words its driver shouted at them; or why, when they speeded up and the second car fell behind, one of the car's occupants shot at them, hitting their son in the head. And Italy did not understand either: did not understand its own violence, simmering up from a feudal past; did not understand the Greens' insistence that they didn't hate Italy for killing their son; above all, did not understand their swift decision to donate all of Nicholas's usable organs for transplant. In this land where a heartless Pope holds sway, organ donation is nearly unheard of, because it is perceived as a violation of the body. As a result most people on transplant lists languish and die. But Nicholas Green's parents had different attitudes, and so his heart and kidneys and liver and eyes were cut out of him, and helicoptered all over the south, and sewn into the bodies of other children. In response Italy venerated the Greens. While some Italian tourists beaten in Miami went into crippling debt to pay their hospital bills, the Greens were given medals by President Oscar Luigi Scalfaro. Prime Minister Silvio Berlusconi arranged for them to be flown home on a military jet. At every café and restaurant people talked about Nicholas Green, and brooded, and blamed themselves. Subsequently the rate of organ donation shot up dramatically.

Around the same time Moana Pozzi died of liver cancer. At thirty-two she was Italy's second most popular porn actress, after Cicciolina, who had achieved brief worldwide fame as a result of being elected to Parliament on the Radical party ticket. Moana had a sturdy dignity somehow at odds with the situations in which her films usually placed her. With her long blonde hair, her severe, equine, almost masculine face, she looked more Scandinavian than Mediterranean: a sort of Liv Ullman for adult video. She was much loved in Italy; the national newspaper *La Repubblica*, in its obituary, emphasized her reputation as "a person of intelligence

and sensitivity." In her capable hands, pornography had become almost respectable, so much so that her sister, Baby Pozzi, was following in her footsteps. Then at the height of her career, according to the papers, she traveled to India and came back with liver cancer. (A link between journey and tumor was cryptically implied.) Five months later she was dead.

But this is not the end of the story. According to her mother, Moana's last wish had been to have her ashes scattered over the sea. The scattering was scheduled to take place, when at the eleventh hour a judge threatened to arrest the Pozzis should they go through with it: in Italy ash-scattering is criminal. Ashes can be kept in urns, or buried. But they cannot be scattered over the earth.

What do these two dead people have to do with each other? I think this: Catholic doctrine disdains life even as it reveres the body (even the cremated body). But Moana insisted life was the body, while the Greens willingly sacked the temple of their child's body so that other children could live. Just as the Pope prepared to publish his cheap-shot book, the organs of life were scattered where ashes cannot be.

When I first read about Nicholas Green, I thought immediately of that very Italian martyr Santa Lucia, whose eyes were gouged out by the pagans, and who in paintings carries those eyes on a plate for eternity to reverence. Now Italy has a new saint, who holds an empty plate. The eyes have gone to save a child from blindness.   — D.L.

We are accustomed to hear the south of Italy spoken of as a beautiful country. Its mountain forms are graceful above others, its sea bays exquisite in outline and hue; but it is only beautiful in superficial aspect. In closer detail it is wild and melancholy. Its forests are sombre-leaved, labyrinth-stemmed; the carubbe, the olive, laurel, and ilex, are alike in that strange feverish twisting of their branches, as if in spasms of half human pain:—Avernus forests; one fears to break their boughs, lest they should cry to us from the rents; the rocks they shade are of ashes, or thrice-molten lava; iron sponge whose every pore has been filled with fire. Silent villages, earthquake shaken, without commerce, without industry, without knowledge, without hope, gleam in white ruin from hillside to hillside; far-winding wrecks of immemorial walls surround the dust of cities long forsaken: the mountain streams moan through the cold arches of their foundations, green with weed, and rage over the heaps of their fallen towers. Far above, in thunder-blue serration, stand the eternal edges of the angry Apennine, dark with rolling impendence of volcanic cloud.

John Ruskin, *Modern Painters* (1856)

*O*n January, the Greens appeared on the cover of a magazine, wishing a happy new year to Italy. The press was still amazed that they had no desire for *vendetta*, did not cling to the notion that blood must have blood. In Italy the very real consolations of revenge are not to be undersold.

A program called *Perdoname*—"Forgive me"— has become extremely popular here in this year of the Greens. People go on this show when they've had disputes with loved ones, and cannot seem to bring those loved ones round to making up with them.

One afternoon a very old man appeared on *Perdoname*. His palsied face recalled that of Benedetto Croce. He wanted forgiveness from his sister—I could not understand exactly what he'd done, since he spoke in a dialect; all I was able to determine was that he had refused to attend both his brother-in-law's and his father's funerals, which in Catholic Italy is pretty unforgivable.

Minicam in hand, *Perdoname*'s roving reporter shows up at the sister's door. "These flowers are from your brother," she says. "He asks that you accept them and with them give him your forgiveness."

The sister, an elegant-looking woman in her fifties, looks pensive, and finally shakes her head. "I cannot accept them," she says. "What he did, it was too strong. He's not bad at heart, but his character is bad."

"His character is bad?"

"He gets too angry. He wouldn't attend my husband's funeral. He wouldn't attend our father's funeral. I'm sorry but I cannot forgive him."

The reporter makes a few more efforts to persuade her, but the sister remains adamant.

We return to the studio. The old man looks at the floor. "She's proud," he keeps murmuring. "She's too proud."

"And what if I were to tell you," the host says, "that your sister was here, in the studio, today?"

The old man lifts his head.

"Yes, she is here," the host says. "Afterwards she had second thoughts. Let's bring her out: Letizia."

Now, like an actress striding down to chat with Johnny Carson, in comes Letizia, beaming while the audience applauds. The old man stands; he embraces her. Tears stream down his twisted face. "She's so beautiful," he says to the host. "So beautiful."

"How could I not forgive him?" the sister says. "He's my brother."

"But you must promise to control your temper, and not be so proud," cautions the host.

"He's bad in character, but his heart is good," the sister says.

"I promise," says the weeping old man.

"Good," the sister says. "Good. And tonight we'll have supper together."

Well, in Italy, this is the best news of all. The audience practically stampedes, it approves so wholeheartedly. Forgiveness—too often cheaply offered and accepted, passed back and forth like a single bunch of flowers that commerce has left listless—is stern, uncompromising, real as flowers; indeed, in its outer aspects, not unlike *vendetta* itself.

It's winter outside but there's an echo of spring in the air, like the scent of perfume lingering in a dead woman's boudoir. Thus spring must have felt to the sufferers in the *Inferno*: a memory of sun that was almost a sunbeam, bleeding through the layers of blackness to those who would never know the real sun again, because they were not forgiven.   — D.L.

*A*mong all the paintings of the annunciation in the Accademia, there is one that calls up Dante's "that day we read no further" *(Inferno)* . . . what *did* the Virgin do after she put down her book on that ancient day? . . . from the Fondamente Nuove, with the hills in the distance looking for all the world like the background of a painting by Giorgione, the cemetery of San Michele promises somber grandeur . . . Stravinsky is buried there; also Diaghilev—among the tributes placed on his grave is a toe shoe—and Baron Corvo, who was, among many other things, a gondolier . . . alas, too many flowers annul the promise: true grandeur cannot exist in the presence of pastels . . . for the forty-eight hours between November 19 and 21, the "Votive Bridge" spans the Grand Canal from the Gritti Palace Hotel to Santa Maria della Salute— the church was built after the plague of 1630–1631 that carried away fifty thousand Venetians . . . three and a half centuries later the Venetians give thanks to the Madonna for their delivery (even though cats imported from Syria, not her, put an end to the plague-carrying rats) . . . Americans give thanks during the same week, except that our tradition calls for turkey and dressing rather than the Venetian *castra-dina*, which is basically corned mutton and cabbage ... each part of Italy has its *dolci tipici*, or "typical sweets" ... perhaps best among them is the Venetian *fritella*—a kind of hush puppy filled with pine nuts and raisins and rolled in crystals of sugar ... Mary McCarthy, in *Venice Observed*, notes that although in 1961 there was a cocktail named for the painter Bellini—invented here at Harry's Bar—as well as for Titian and Giorgione, there was not one named for Tintoretto; there is now (pomegranate juice and *prosecco*) ... in the Treasury of San Marco is a glass paten from Constantinople in a pattern known in English as honeycomb, and in Italian as *nido d'ape* (bee's nest) ... the mosaics of the Basilica of San Marco, in the late afternoon, take on the woolly quality of tapestry ... always the floors of San Marco astound; meticulous, Byzantine figurations approximated in America only on old quilts ... finally porphyry, the most gratefully tactile of all stone; the substance of the four embracing figures ("The Four Moors") at the entrance to the Doges' Palace.

— M.M.

One can forgive a place three thousand miles from Italy for not being Italian; but that a village on the very border should remain stolidly, immovably Swiss was a constant source of exasperation. Even the landscape had neglected its opportunities. A few miles off it became the accomplice of man's most exquisite imaginings; but here we could see in it only endless material for Swiss clocks and fodder.

The trouble began with our watching the diligences. Every evening we saw one toiling up the pass from Chiavenna, with dusty horses and perspiring passengers. How we pitied those passengers! We walked among them puffed up with all the good air in our lungs. We felt fresh and cool and enviable, and moralized on the plaintive lot of those whose scant holidays compelled them to visit Italy in August. But already the poison was at work. We pictured what our less fortunate brothers had seen till we began to wonder if, after all, they were less fortunate. At least they had *been there;* and what drawbacks could qualify that fact? Was it better to be cool and look at a water-fall, or to be hot and look at Saint Mark's? Was it better to walk on gentians or on mosaic, to smell fir-needles or incense? Was it, in short, ever well to be elsewhere when one might be in Italy?

Edith Wharton, *Italian Backgrounds* (1905)

Dulcis in fondo

Two excerpts from *Sea and Sardinia* by D. H. Lawrence.
First published by Thomas Seltzer, Inc., 1921.
Reprinted by permission of Laurence Pollinger Ltd on
behalf of the Estate of Frieda Lawrence Ravagli. Excerpt
from *The Renaissance* by Walter Pater. First printed by
Macmillan, London, 1873, reprinted in 1978. Excerpt
from *Melodies and Memories* by Nellie Melba. First print-
ed in 1925 by Thorton Butterworth, Ltd. Excerpt from
The Gallery by John Horne Burns. Copyright © 1947 by
John Horne Burns. Reprinted by permission of the
William Morris Agency, Inc. on behalf of the Author.
Excerpt from *Remarks on Antiquities, Arts and Letters
During an Excursion in Italy in the Years 1802 and 1803*
by Joseph Forsyth, Esq., published by P. G. LeDouble,
1813. Excerpt from *The Innocents Abroad* by Mark
Twain. First published by American Publishing Co.,
1869. Excerpt from *The Surprise of Cremona* by Edith
Templeton. Copyright © 1954 by Edith Templeton.
Reprinted with permission of Edith Templeton. Excerpt
from *Memoirs of Hadrian* by Marguerite Yourcenar,
translated by Grace Frick. Copyright © 1963 by
Marguerite Yourcenar. Copyright renewed © 1991 by
Editions Gallimard. Reprinted by kind permission of
Reed Books. Excerpt from *Venice Observed* by Mary
McCarthy. Copyright © 1961 Estate of Mary
McCarthy. Reprinted with permission of A. M. Heath &
Co. Ltd. Excerpt from a letter to Ethel Smyth as repro-
duced in *The Cosmopolites* by Harry Brewster. Copyright
© 1994 by Harry Brewster. Reprinted with permission
of Harry Brewster. Excerpt from *Old Calabria* by
Norman Douglas. First printed by Martin Secker in
1915. Excerpt from *Conducted Tour* by Bernard Levin.

INDEX